HAUNTED ASHEVILLE

Also by Joshua P. Warren

Joshua Warren's Gallery of Mystery & Suspense

Speaking of Strange...

Plausible Ghosts

HAUNTED ASHEVILLE

by *Joshua P. Warren*

With Special Photographs by Mark-Ellis Bennett

and Graphical Effects by Tim Pedersen

**SHADOWBOX
PUBLICATIONS**

a division of Shadowbox Enterprises

cover design by Tim Pedersen

cover photographs by Joshua P. Warren

Pink Lady cover model: Ashley E. Simpson

Alice model: Patricia Gonzalez

10 9 8 7 6

ISBN 0-9649370-2-6

Printed in the United States of America

SHADOWBOX PUBLICATIONS
a division of Shadowbox Enterprises
P.O. Box 16801
Asheville, NC 28816

In remembrance of Dr. Deryl Howard, who shared my interest in the world of the unknown.

Warren

ACKNOWLEDGMENTS

Those following helped to publicize or produce this book and research in some form which is greatly appreciated:

Craig Madison & Dave Tomsky, The Grove Park Inn
Bill Banner & the staff of 13 WLOS TV
Wayne Kinser, Peppertree Resorts
Marge Turcot, The Reed House
Larry Pope & Lydia Carrington, *The Asheville Citizen-Times*
Charles Yost, Dynamic Systems, Inc.
Bill Ladu & Richard Jones, Erwin High School
Ann Wright & Zoe Rhine, Pack Memorial Library
Tim Daniels, UNCA's Ramsey Library
Mitzi Tessier
Lou Harshaw
Milton Ready
April Boulware...

...And all those names mentioned within this book, as well as the very many anonymous people who patiently answered my endless questions. Without their generous cooperation, this book would have never been.

Warren

TABLE OF CONTENTS

"Men fear death as children fear to go in the dark; and as that natural fear in children is increased with tales, so is the other."

~Francis Bacon
(1561 – 1626)

Warren

INTRODUCTION

Things die slowly in the mountains. Perhaps it's the rocks, or the streams. Perhaps it's the thick forests, or the misty clouds that lie low on the horizon. Perhaps it's the chill in the air, or the way the pale moon gleams down on the rolling hillsides. Whether basking in the warmth of a July sun, or trudging through the banks of a thick January snow— *things die slowly in the mountains.*

There is something about the spirit that tends to linger here. There is something about the dark, looming mountains that envelops the soul and entices it to stay. To walk among them is to feel the scope of the ages. For no mountain is exactly what it seems to be. Each one is a collage—an aggregation—of all that has passed through it. Each Native American who smoked a pipe by a crackling campfire; each peaceful deer that drank from a pond beneath the starry sky; and each pioneer who carved his way through the rugged terrain, has left a mark. Those who have lived in the mountains each left traces of themselves across the timeless ranges— not to mention those who *died* there.

What are the mountains without the mountain people? It is they, in their small towns, who have cherished the protection of nature's greatest barriers. They have defined the meaning of genuine culture among the elements, and learned to harness the power of the land. What more delicate and painstakingly crafted monuments can one find than within the heart of a mountain town? Such towns are built on true sweat, blood, and tears. Even though they may generally have eluded the spotlight through time, they have progressed while maintaining their integrity and authenticity. Such towns are found scattered here and there all about the Appalachians. And although each one shares a legacy and kinship with the other, who can find a finer example than the city of Asheville?

For a small mountain town, Asheville has seen its share of action. From its earliest days as a rough pioneer town, to its boom days and beyond, Asheville has, in some respects, broken the mold of the simple mountain town. Although it remains a cool oasis of scenic grandeur and relaxation, much has happened here. There is a special tradition within the mountains of Asheville that has sunken deep within the roots of its people. It was the *only* place in the world which drew George Vanderbilt to build his illustrious home. It was the *only* place in the world suitable for E.W. Grove to realize his dream of constructing the world's finest resort. It was the *only* place in the world that Thomas Wolfe immortalized again and again in his prolific writings. Yes, truly, Asheville has made a name for itself.

Yet, with the all the bustling that has taken place in the forefront of Asheville's development, the mountains remain, standing silently in the background. They soak up the hearts of the people to their dark majesty, and when the people die, they surely leave a piece of themselves behind. But, then again, *some die more slowly than others*. It is from these spirits—these souls that linger on a bit longer than the rest—that come the stories.

You know the ones...the ones about the lost spirits wandering restlessly. They are most always searching for something. Maybe they search for peace, a lost lover, or to exact vengeance upon those who wronged them in life. Chances are, however, they will never find it. With all their immortal abilities and ancient years of ceaseless searching, they still cannot find what they are looking for. Why? Because then they would go away—*and we won't let them.*

They are the classic howls on a windy night, or an icy hand laid upon your back in an empty room. They are the faint whisper you thought may have called your name—but then again, no—certainly it must be "just your imagination." They are the shadows that dance around a campfire at night, and though we may sometimes dread them, deep inside we cannot live without them. To us, they represent more than just a cold chill or a shudder in the dark. Deep inside the recesses of our souls we are fascinated by them because they symbolize the unknown.

Our knowledge can sometimes imprison us. Because of gravity, we know we cannot spread our arms and fly. Because of light, we cannot make ourselves invisible. Because of mass, we cannot walk through walls—but they can. And even though they seem to be imprisoned by some forces beyond our knowledge, to us they seem so free. They represent a vast blackness of unseen possibilities, and the unseen possibilities are the breeding ground of hope. Therefore, on some deep, subconscious level, perhaps the ghost symbolizes hope itself. Perhaps it embodies the excitement of discovery and the challenging fascination of the mystery. There are no wrong answers when the answers are not known. Since the ghost is the personality of the enigma, it seems to be a limitless slate upon which we may project our hopes, fears, and ideas, restricted only by the boundaries of our imaginations. That is why we won't let them go away.

With this, it seems obvious why the notion of the ghost has remained popular since the dawn of mankind. But still, as much as we enjoy the stories, they're still just stories— *right?* There are some, however, who say the story is just the beginning. As a matter of fact, many of those people live in Asheville. They are people, usually just as sane as you and I *(heh, heh)* who, in many cases, didn't really believe in ghosts until, one night (or day as it may be) everything changed. While strolling in the Grove Park Inn, or walking under Helen's Bridge, "something" happened...Not often, mind you...As a matter of fact, very rarely. But, then again, it takes only one time to change your mind (and, perhaps, your britches). Unfortunately, most of us will never get to see these ghosts. We will only hear the stories that continue to be passed down through the generations. But where, if we trace back through time, did the stories begin? We all know who supposedly died, but how can we find out who *really* died? When will someone take the time to research and question, and find out the facts behind the stories? Well, guess what: *Someone finally did.*

Records around these parts are terribly scant, as anyone who has researched in Asheville knows. But there are some goodies out there, just waiting to be saved before they decay in some forgotten file drawer. There are mainly bits and pieces, scattered here and there. It's like a big puzzle, or a recently unearthed mountain skeleton. I've tried to reassemble as many authentic bones as I could find, but, like an archaeologist, had to fill in the gaps with "plaster parts" (in this case, insubstantial legend).

There are usually a number of possibilities that arise when it comes to finding the source of a legend. Sometimes weird things happen, like the same name popping up in different legends. Around Asheville, two names that seem to recur quite frequently in ghost stories are Helen and Alice. In this book, you'll read about real people in Asheville, who died tragically, by both those names. The relationships between the real people and the stories are debatable, however. In some cases it seems as though there may have originally been no authentic connection. However, when a person tragically dies in the area, that person's name seems to stick in the public memory. Perhaps, if one were looking for the name of an anonymous ghost, one such name would seem to be a likely candidate. All in all, some interesting coincidences do seem to arise.

On a more superstitious note, you will also notice the number 13 shows up in the darndest of places. You will also find, as with most ghost stories, that majority of the unrestful spirits are women. One may only speculate as to the reason for this.

"Well all that's fine and good," says that rational voice from our intellectual nature, "but where's the evidence?" Stories come a dime a dozen and eyewitnesses can be unreliable. So what's left over for the armchair critic? That is where I step in with the marvelous gizmos of technology, and delve into the science of ghost hunting.

To put it in a nutshell, aside from all the flesh, people are energy. When the flesh is gone, the energy (which can be neither created nor destroyed) is left over. This energy seems to be the ghost. Since the mind (considered very different from the brain) is also energy, it retains the consciousness of the person. In other words, the energy is the real you. You are not literally rotting away in the coffin. This would explain why, whenever a ghost is encountered, there is a huge fluctuation of electromagnetic energy. Keeping this in mind, we try to scientifically study a ghost from the perspective of studying energy fields.

I don't mean to get too technical on you, but, since they are included throughout the book, I'll give a quick overview of some equipment used to study ghosts. Regular 35mm cameras are used more than anything. In many cases, one may not actually see a ghost, but takes a photograph of a haunted place. Later, when it is developed, a strange image appears. It seems that these high concentrations of electromagnetic fields may directly affect the emulsion of the film. Though they may be out of our visible range, the camera can somehow pick them up. By the use of special films and filters, cameras can also be made to photograph into the infrared and ultraviolet range. Such photography can be likened to taking x-rays. Though energy may not be viewed at the time of the photograph, it appears after developing. This simply broadens the possibility of capturing a significant image. Inaudible noises can be imprinted directly on audio tape according to the same principle.

An electromagnetic field meter is also more than handy to have on the scene. These are obviously used to detect such energy masses. Many times, when an energy fluctuation is present, a photograph taken will yield odd images.

Night vision devices can also be efficiently employed. Aside from their use in viewing areas in darkness, they allow the viewer to see into the infrared range.

Wimshurst and Van de Graff generators are electrostatic devices which disperse ions into the air. It is believed that the materialization of a ghost is accompanied by a massive concentration of ions correlating with the electromagnetic energy. Using devices which generate ion concentrations may enhance supernatural activity.

A Tesla Coil is one of the most fascinating electrodynamic devices available. It emits high frequency electrical oscillations. When properly employed, it can alter the ionic and electromagnetic environment in a number of ways.

These are just a few of the devices employed in paranormal (meaning *beyond* normal) research. You must realize that, when studying the unknown, a number of techniques must be utilized. We don't necessarily know if what we're studying should fall under physics, biology, psychology, etc. Therefore, we must combine instruments and procedures from each science until we pinpoint exactly what we're looking for. Such instrumentation was not employed while researching for every chapter in this book. You will see it mentioned here and there, though. I won't bog you down with the technical parts of ghost research. However, if you are scientifically interested in paranormal research, you should certainly read *Plausible Ghosts*, my third book (also available from SHADOWBOX PUBLICATIONS).

All in all, I've tried to include a little something for everyone in this book. There are legends, never before published historical facts, eyewitness accounts, and scientific data. On top of that, the book contains a generous portion of photographs. Aside from photographs obtained during research, special photographs of most locations featured were made by Mark-Ellis Bennett. Special ghostly effects were done by Tim Pedersen. Both men are nationally renowned for their work. I should mention that, unless otherwise marked, the photographer of each picture is denoted by the name printed below the photo.

ASHEVILLE IS FULL OF HAUNTED PLACES. This book just includes some of the most fascinating. You'll find that the Pink Lady of the Grove Park Inn is the feature of this book, however. This is because I was hired by the Grove Park Inn to research the phenomenon independently. Therefore, that research project was the biggest on which I had ever embarked. I have no doubt that you'll find the combination of lore, sightings, and data compelling, at very least. I am, however, sorry to say there are a number of other intriguing places in Asheville, privately owned, where the present owners do not want their legends publicized. It is a shame to see such good stories go to waste. Maybe after this book, they'll come around.

But enough from me! The suspense has been created, the drum roll has been completed, and now it's time for you to explore the darker side of Asheville. You are about to embark on a journey to places in Asheville you always wanted to go at night, but were usually too afraid. Never fear, I've done it for you. Full moons and graveyards seem to be my cup of tea. And, as you read, if a cold shudder suddenly runs up your spine, pay it no attention. I've probably just walked across *your* grave.

There are haunting tales waiting to be told in the pages ahead. Read them carefully. Take your time. Things die slowly in the mountains—*especially stories.*

Warren

THE PINK LADY
OF THE GROVE PARK INN

THE LEGEND...

The November night was crisp and cold. A hint of smoke drifted in the thin air of the hotel's Palm Court, as mammoth fireplaces roared in the Great Hall, two floors below. The blaze from the fire sent forth a jovial warmth that mingled with the nature of the guests, merrily conversing before it. A jazzy, 1920s tune bounced around the massive stones and pillars of the hall, as chuckles and murmured conversation filled the center of the mighty hotel. She could hear them from the fifth floor of the Palm Court—a desolate place that night.

She was young and beautiful—a slender neck and graceful features. Her long, lustrous hair fell around the shoulders of the pink evening gown she'd worn for the special night. She was such a pretty girl, but why did she seem so melancholy? Her bright eyes sparkled as she stared from the edge of the fifth floor. From such a height, the tiles far below seemed so strangely welcoming. It was almost as though they beckoned to her. They called her name in a soft whisper—and she was drawn. It was such a subtle moment—such a quiet moment. She was hypnotized by the expanse below. The danger must have registered somewhere in her mind, but she ignored it. *She was drawn.*

The security of the low wall was there, holding her back. It was trying to tell her "No! No! There is danger here! Lean back!" But the warning fell on deaf ears. The hugeness of the room invited her to join. The air, even in its thinness, seemed strong enough to support her. She rested upon it more and more. Her arms reached for it, farther and farther. A silent crescendo arose in the sky, and then, at once, the strength of the floor below her dainty feet was there no more.

What had happened? Had she shifted her weight too far? Had a malicious force shoved her *just enough?* Had she seen the cure to her depression on the cold floor far below?

It was like slow motion—the wind rushing through her thick hair one last time; her long, pink gown pressed against her body by the air that had sworn to support her. The spell had been broken. Her enchantment was now gone—but it was too late. The floor became larger and larger as the tiles she was to swiftly meet showed their hardness once again. Horror flashed in her deep eyes. A scream arose in her delicate throat, but there was no time for it to escape. One last impression: the laughs, the murmurs, the smoke, the music, the chill in the air, the hardness of the floor—and then, *the impact.*

In the Great Hall, the conversation didn't flinch. The band didn't miss a note. The fireplace kept right on burning as brightly and warmly as ever. But something had changed. Everyone knew it. No one could quite place it. No one even mentioned it. But they knew it had changed. It was a sort of new weight on their shoulders.

A ghost of a grimace showed behind their smiles. But what was it? What had caused this new sensation? They would find out later that night.

The moon would show brightly when they entered the silence of the Palm Court. There, they would find the pale girl, in her shapely, pink gown, as cold and lifeless as the tiles. Then, they would know: *Tragedy.* It was tragedy that had weighed so heavy in the air of the Grove Park Inn that chilly night.

TIME WOULD PASS, and the night would become forgotten. The body would disintegrate in the soil, along with the pink gown. The hardened bones of the pitiful lady would disappear, but *something* seemed to be left behind. At first, no one knew exactly what it was. But they continued to hear the stories.

"I've seen it," someone would say. "I've seen it with my own eyes. I was working late one night, up there in the Main Inn. It was quiet, and there was no one else around. Then, all at once, I got the strangest feeling I wasn't alone anymore. I felt like someone was watching me when my head was turned the other way. This sort o' chill went up my spine, and the hair began to stand on the back of my neck. I got a real cold shiver, and when I looked up, there she was—just standin' there. It was a lady in a long pink dress. She seemed sad and dreary—maybe even a little bit lost. And then, almost as soon as I'd seen her, she just disappeared into thin air. It was like she was never there."

Generation after generation, the stories continued to pour from the massive walls of the Grove Park Inn. Someone would see her from a distance, gliding across a hallway. Someone else would round a corner and meet her face to face, just before she would vanish. And then there were the mischievous things... Someone would buzz the elevator to the fifth floor, but the operator, much to his surprise, would answer the call to meet an empty hallway. Vacant rooms would be locked from the inside, and hotel lights would turn on and off with seemingly no controlling hand in sight.

Bellmen, maids, doctors, chiefs of police—children and adults—the experiences spanned all walks of life. "There's a ghost in the Grove Park Inn!" some would exclaim, as though it was a *bad* thing. Hotel administration forbade conversation of the topic to avoid frightening guests. But many more people, who had picked up the story in rumor, came to the timeless inn with the hopes of catching a glimpse themselves. Some did. Most did not. But still, once in a blue moon, a lucky someone would see her. And those who did, in that single instance that they saw the phantom glide away, realized once and for all its significance to the Grove Park. In most places, people come and people go. History presents itself and then dies away forever. But not in the Grove Park Inn. The past—the hotel's rich, historical integrity is as alive and active as ever. It literally roams the halls. And what better a place to spend eternity than within the walls of the world's greatest resort?

Her identity remains a mystery. Her very existence is shrouded with mystique. She is elusive, forlorn, and benevolent. She is beautiful, yet sad. She is welcomed by many, but feared by a few. To those who see her often, she is a peaceful and comforting sight, yet even to

Warren

The view from one level of the Palm Court

them, she remains an enigma. Misunderstood, yet timeless, she is an integral part of the culture of the Grove Park Inn. The mere mention of her name will wrinkle a furrowed brow and revive a thousand dusty stories. The workers of the Grove Park Inn know her all too well. They call her simply, the *Pink Lady*.

======================

...And so goes the most familiar legend of the Grove Park Inn. Since its construction by E.W. Grove in 1913, the famous hotel has seen a countless number of personalities. Safeguarding guests from Thomas Edison, Henry Ford, and F. Scott Fitzgerald, to Harry Houdini, Franklin D. Roosevelt, and Richard Nixon, the Grove Park Inn has become a twentieth century American time capsule. To simply wander through the halls of the granite wonder is to lose oneself in the nostalgic past. There is more to say about the place than one book could possibly ever hold. In any case, it may be quite safely assumed that if the most beloved person in the world came to Asheville, he or she would stay at the Grove Park Inn.

It should come as no surprise that a dwelling such as this would have its own ghosts. Since, at very least, the 1940s, reports of strange occurrences have poured from the hotel. Bill and Mildred Nielson each worked at the hotel for over forty years. Mrs. Nielson recalled an experience her husband had one night around 1940. "One time, when he was a night watchman there, he was makin' his rounds... and when he started back somebody just took him by the arm, and held him by the arm till he got back to the hotel lobby... He looked to see, but there was no one there."

Stories like that of the Nielsons' are typical of the hotel. In the past, the hotel closed down for the winter months. During these times, when the hotel was vacant except for a few employees, some of the strangest occurrences were reported. It was commonplace for the elevator to be buzzed to the fourth or fifth floors of the Main Inn when only two people were in the hotel, both in the Great Hall.

Freda Baker, who has worked in Catering and Convention Services at the hotel for over seventeen years, once had a strange experience in 1981. While the hotel was closed down in the winter, she was there one night reprogramming some cash registers and completing preparatory errands. She was the only person in the hotel, and a single security guard was somewhere outside the building.

Around 11 p.m., she exited the inn and, since the door locked behind her, could not get back inside. Baker went to her car, but was unable to leave due to a chain across the hotel driveway. At that point, she looked up and saw all the lights on the sixth floor of the Main Inn turned on. Naturally, she assumed the security officer was on the sixth floor. Baker then pulled her car in front of the hotel and began honking the horn in hopes of getting the officer's attention. After a few moments, the officer came walking up through the parking lot. Puzzled that he was not inside the hotel, Baker wondered why the lights were on. She and the officer entered the building and went to the sixth floor. When they arrived, however, all the lights were off.

At a loss for an explanation, the officer escorted her

back to her car. Once outside, the pair looked up at the towering, dark hotel. Baker will never forget what suddenly happened. "Every single light—we're talking *every single sleeping room light*—came on at the same time."

In her many years at the hotel, Baker has grown used to a number of small unexplained occurrences. "You'll hear doors close and doors open, and there's not a soul up here but you. They're friendly though," she says of the spirits. "They don't ever bother anybody."

The Pink Lady is, without a doubt, the most popular spectre reported in the hotel. It is understandable that those who see or experience her should have mixed reactions of the encounter. As for the occurrences themselves, however, they are always benevolent and, at very most, mischievous. The peacefulness associated with the spirit is well known to Pat Franklin, the manager of Elaine's, the Grove Park Inn's nightclub.

"It's a real gentle spirit, whatever it is," said Franklin. She has encountered what she believes to be a form of the Pink Lady on several occasions. "It's like a real dense smoke," she says of the apparition. "It just kind o' flows. It's kind of a pinkish pastel." On one occasion, when the club was full, Franklin was walking towards the landing of the steps and had to suddenly dodge to prevent walking into the spirit. Stories such as this seem to illustrate the sociable side of the classic ghost.

To Franklin, as well as some others who have seen the Pink Lady, the spirit appears as an abstract, foggy form. However in many other cases, the spirit appears to be an almost tangible, distinct figure of a young woman. It was this impression that Carol Cline Rice,

Warren

Pat Franklin

and a fellow coworker, received one night.

Carol Cline Rice has worked at the Grove Park Inn for eight years. One New Year's Eve of 1989, Mrs. Rice and a lady coworker attended a party at the hotel's accounting office. It was between three and four in the morning, and they were the only ones left after the party had wound down. "We heard someone come in the back door," she said. "We looked up and somebody went by real fast. It was a woman. She was dressed in kind of party clothes. We thought it was a guest, so both of us got up, and then she was gone. We didn't know where she went so we called security. They came and looked but they couldn't find her."

Sharon Ponder was a photographer at the Grove Park Inn from 1991 to 1995. She claims while working in her photo lab in the Old Plantation kitchen, she encountered the distinct form of the phantom several times. "I encountered her probably four times. She used to play tricks on me... She'd move things around on me, and she touched me a couple of times... I saw her a couple of times. She used to scare my photographers."

Ponder had been working at the times the Pink Lady tapped her on the back. "It felt cold," she said of the phantom's touch. "It makes your hair stand up on end... like, in a really bad electrical storm, right before the lightning strikes, your hair stands on end. But it was cold—icy."

On one occasion, Ponder entered the room and glimpsed the Pink Lady standing by a window. When Ponder looked back, she was gone. Late one night, Ponder was working when she looked up at the window. In the dark glass, she could see the Pink Lady standing in the doorway behind her. When she turned around, the phantom had vanished once again.

"One time that I saw her she was dressed in baby blues; she wasn't dressed in pink. The other time I saw her she was dressed in pink. She seemed to have dark hair as far as I could tell... Most of the time I didn't see her, I just knew she was there."

The Pink Lady also often moved Ponder's materials around mischievously. "All my photographers were afraid of her... To me, she was more of a prankster. She liked to play tricks. She liked to have contact. She liked to let me know that she was there. But I think once she realized that I couldn't be frightened, that she didn't bother me, it seemed like I didn't have as many encounters with her... I was never afraid of her—*ever*."

The Pink Lady has also visually presented herself to guests. It seems as though children are a particular favorite of the ghost. In 1993, the hotel received a letter from a doctor who lived in Tampa, Florida. He and his family had stayed in rooms 443 and 445 in December of 1992. One afternoon, while the doctor and his wife were out, his two-year-old son napped in room 443, while a baby sitter stayed in room 445. The baby sitter heard the child murmuring for approximately an hour and a half before falling asleep. When the sitter went in to check on him, the child turned to ask, "Where did the nice lady go?" The puzzled sitter asked him what lady he was talking about. "The nice lady I've been talking to," was his reply. The sitter tucked him in and left the room. He murmured around ten more minutes before falling asleep. When the doctor and his wife returned, the child told them of the "nice lady." The incident repeated itself the following afternoon. On both days, the doctor was sure he had chained and locked the door.

As can be seen from some of the previous examples, descriptions of the Pink Lady can vary from sighting to sighting. From abstract to distinct, from brunette to blond, from pink clothes to blue ones, the apparition dons many masks. But then, the question arises, is the same spirit always seen? Although the Pink Lady is the dominant spirit at the hotel, there have been reports of more than one spectre being seen at the same time.

Nancy Fulham worked at Elaine's for five years. She would often see several dark, abstract forms at various parts of the hotel. Sometimes, out of the corner of her eye, she would see what she perceived to be security coming off the elevator (outside of Elaine's) in dark suits. Then, the forms would vanish. "I'd see them all over the hotel," she said. "I would have assumed that they were men in dark suits. They were really kind of comical, too. I would get the impression that they would be right behind somebody else, kind of walking just like that person... kind of pranksterish. The only female one—the only time I ever encountered that one was down in the nightclub. And that was really just kind of like a light, with no real shape or form or anything that I noticed." Fulham said the female one seemed to project an aura of light pastel pink or yellow. She never felt afraid of any of the apparitions she saw.

Another Grove Park employee, who had reservations about publicizing her name, has seen these mysterious, dark phantoms many times as well. "The only ones I've seen have been down at Elaine's, actually," she said. "There's quite a few people that have seen them... they

Downtown Asheville in 1913 (courtesy the Ewart M. Ball Collection, Ramsey Library, UNC-Asheville)

don't really have any particular physical shape other than being more shadowy looking. There's black ones down there and there's white ones. I have seen the black ones go by. It's almost like seeing something that's darker than what's there moving through the room. There's several people you could talk to about them, but they are not related to the Pink Lady. It's like a dark shadow moving through the place."

Bill Kelley has worked at the hotel since 1988. Though he is now the Director of Training, he was previously the Director of Security. In that position, he became very aware of strange happenings in and around the hotel. He would often hear reports of the phantoms around Elaine's.

"They have a glass elevator that goes down to Elaine's," said Kelley. "Some of the servers or bartenders that would work down there would report that one of the bartenders would bus the bar and the other one would take the trash up in the elevator, and then they would come back down again. In that process, when they came down to Elaine's level, the bartender that was in Elaine's could see the back of the glass elevator. He could see a silhouette in there with the other bartender. The bartender would come out and the silhouette wouldn't come out. The silhouette would disappear and, of course, the bartender that was in the elevator had no knowledge that somebody was standing behind him."

In the mornings at the hotel, Kelley would also often hear children speak of the lady in pink they had seen the previous night. Though their parents would usually humor them, Kelley knew exactly what they were talking about.

Although the reports of sightings poured from the hotel, there were many more reports of odd occurrences which lacked a conventional explanation. "On a couple of different occasions, as security, we had to go up in the Main Inn and unlock bathroom doors," said Kelley, "understanding the bathroom doors bolt from the *inside*. There's no key that gets them open. The only way that one could lock those things would be from the inside. So we had to go up there and take the hinges off the door to get the doors open."

Kelley also talked of the trouble he had staffing the hotel's Country Club, a short distance from the Main Inn. According to Kelley, everyone thought it was haunted due to strange activities (the elevator going up and down by itself at three in the morning, doors opening themselves, and occasional sightings of a pink silhouette moving across the area). Kelley eventually got one man to staff the club for three years. The man virtually stayed at the Country Club all the time, never coming to the Main Inn. After the man retired, Kelley put electronics in the building. "It seemed from that point we started getting reportings up in the main hotel. I guess because there was no one down there to play with anymore. She decided to come up to the main hotel."

The elusive ghosts of the Grove Park Inn may only visually present themselves on special occasions. However, unusual and mischievous events often take place in guests' rooms at night. Bob Morris, the Chief of Police at Kitty Hawk, North Carolina, will attest to that fact.

Morris stayed in room 448 the night of February 6, 1996. He was attending a Chiefs of Police Conference in the hotel. After arriving at the hotel around 6:30 in the evening, he went directly to his room. After entering, Chief Morris sat down on his bed, with his back to the door, and picked up the telephone to call his wife. "I was sitting there waiting for the ring," Morris recalled, "and— you know how it feels when somebody sits on a bed that you're sittin' on? How it gives? I experienced that. *Somebody sat on the bed*—that's what I thought. I turned around and looked and nobody was there." After making sure the room was, indeed, vacant, Morris checked the bed to make sure it was solid, and that all the springs were in good shape. The bed seemed to be in very good condition.

The next evening, Morris and a fellow chief were socializing with some vendors at the bar in the Great Hall. One of them asked Morris what he thought about the "ghost." Having no knowledge of supernatural lore in the hotel, Morris inquired, "What ghost?"

"The one on the fourth floor," was the reply.

Morris considered this reply to be too specific. Suspicious he was being "set up" for a practical joke by the fellow chief, Morris grinned. The vendor assured him it was not a joke and scurried away, only to return with a newspaper article about the Pink Lady.

After reading the article, the fellow chief voiced that he knew where to get more information. He then visited the bartender. The bartender referred him to another employee who had supposedly seen the ghost. The employee told the chief of seeing apparitions on several occasions.

As Chief Morris recalled, "I just got a real cold chill that went up my spine at that point, because that whole thing came back to me. I had commented to him when I came back down that first evening, after experiencing that—I said, *'This damn place is haunted'.*" Morris made the magnitude of his experience very clear. "I was *convinced* someone had sat on that bed... it gave substantially."

If it was indeed the Pink Lady who sat on Chief Morris' bed, then it seems the phantom was having a particularly busy night. It was on that same night that Gwen White, President of the National Federation of Press Women, experienced strange phenomena in room 441.

Before leaving for dinner that evening, White and her female roommate were certain the room's closet door was closed and the lights were out. However, when they returned from dinner, the door was open and the lights were on. Since they were already familiar with the Pink Lady lore, they joked about the unexplainable occurrence and went on about their business.

White also said they made a point to leave the bathroom door completely open so that it touched the wall. This would insure that if they had to visit the room during the night, they would not run into the door. Throughout the night, both women did, indeed, visit the bathroom and the door was wide open. However, when they awoke the next morning, the door was completely closed and latched.

Something even stranger happened to White during the night, however. "During the night," she recalled, "I heard a couple of sounds, but I kept saying, 'You're listening for things, you're listening for things, Gwen.' But during the night it was hot in there... I sleep on top of the covers... And my foot was tickled. And so I sorta just moved, with my toe, up against my other foot. And then, in a few minutes, a finger tickled my other foot again. And I looked over and Ellen [her roommate] was in bed fast asleep, so I got under the covers."

Both Chief Bob Morris and Gwen White were staying on the fourth floor of the Main Inn that night. It seems that many reports have emanated from this floor of the hotel. It was on that same floor that Michael White, a previous Grove Park bellman, may have once had a runin with the supernatural.

One night White escorted a guest to his room around four in the morning. On his way back, White recalls what he experienced. "When I turned that corner, it was like I hit something—dead air—and it stopped me and knocked me back against the other wall. I thought I hit a person, but there wasn't a soul anywhere on the floor... I had the sensation I touched somebody."

The fifth floor of the hotel has also been home to many strange experiences. There are some rooms on this floor that hotel employees actually refuse to enter. Aside from the rash of experiences that emanate from the fourth and fifth floors, sightings and weird occurrences are commonplace all throughout the hotel.

Brenda Pace works in the hotel's Convention Services. Although she has never seen a ghost, she says the typewriter in her office has an interesting habit. "It just types when it wants to," she said. In its random spurts of "unattended" typing, the electric machine has produced everything from a few characters to entire incoherent paragraphs.

Pace has worked at the hotel for two years, and says the typing phenomenon had been going on before she started. "We've taken it to the shop twice and they've not been able to figure out what it is. It's in the shop right now for that."

Pace said the typewriter demonstrates such strange activity in "spells." So far, the specialists at the shop have not been able to explain the phenomenon. "They've said they cleaned it up and there's nothing mechanically wrong with it, and they send it back."

Many of the events attributed to the haunting are of such a menial nature. It is in only the most extreme cases that there are reports of employees quitting jobs, and guests asking to be moved to different rooms in the night, due to spectral encounters.

Alec Cantrell, who has worked at the Grove Park Inn for five years, used to be the second and third shift supervisor at the hotel. He remembers an experience an employee reportedly had four or five years ago.

"We were cleaning the Blue Ridge restaurant and he was cleaning some windows, up on a ladder... He said that a woman came by and said 'I'm not workin' you too hard am I, son?' Then she disappeared. I guess somebody had been telling him about the Pink Lady. He went down and clocked out and he hasn't been back since."

Another incident where the ghost interfered with hotel operations is related by Belle Marshall, who works in hotel telecommunications. She remembers an encounter a plumber had in the tunnels under the Main Inn (when it was being redone). He was apparently underground working on some pipes. "He claimed that he was down there and was working, and she [the Pink

Lady] came up to him and hung around him. It scared him so bad he never would go back down there."

FOR SO MANY YEARS, the Grove Park Inn attempted to shield reports of first hand experiences with the supernatural. In November of 1995, however, the hotel decided to officially recognize the phenomena in 1996. For that purpose, I, the author, was hired by the hotel to officially research the phenomena. My findings were to be the subject of a media release in the fall of 1996.

Aside from journalistic investigation, I conducted field research at the hotel from December 29, 1995 to May 27, 1996. During that period, I spent ten nights staying in twenty rooms at the Grove Park Inn. Three colleagues worked with me on an irregular basis throughout the research.

Mark-Ellis Bennett, a specialist in infrared and ultraviolet photography, worked with me most of all. Bennett is also a restoration artist at the hotel. His credits include restoration of the Palm Court and repainting, and stenciling, of the ceiling in the Great Hall. Tim Vandenberghe, who specializes in night vision and acts as a general technician, assisted in the field research of the hotel from December to March. He is the only researcher to ever see a possible apparition with the naked eye. Tim Pedersen, a general technician and noted graphic artist, was present when two of the most significant photographs of the investigation were made.

Even on our first night of investigation, we detected unexplainable fields of electromagnetic energy fluctuating throughout the hotel. There was no conventional explanation for the source of these fields. Throughout the remainder of the research, inexplicable fields of such energy could be detected on a fairly regular basis.

The first photograph that was immediately noted for obtaining a strange image was taken at approximately 5:30 a.m. on December 30, 1995, in the Great Hall. I had inadvertently photographed a chair in the Great Hall with a 35mm camera using Kodak 1000 speed film. When the photo developed, an uncanny gray mist was shown hovering over the chair. It appeared that the film had detected something which my naked eyes had not. The photograph was studied by four photographic experts who could offer no conventional explanation for what caused the ghostly image.

On January 4, 1996, Mark-Ellis Bennett was looking over some photographs taken the night of December 29, 1995. One of them was a picture of the author and Tim Pedersen standing on the fifth floor of the Palm Court. We had posed for the shot, taken by an elevator operator, in order to commemorate the first night of research. However, in the background, towards the right side of the picture, Bennett noticed a strange orangish light glowing outside of room 545. We immediately decided to investigate the room and, after locating it, obtained a maid's key to gain access. *(Note: At the Grove Park Inn, the keys are plastic cards which are inserted into an electronic slot on the door.)*

We inserted the key into the slot, and then pulled it out in the prescribed fashion. However, the door did not unlock. We continued this several times, each time the lock refusing to give us access. We then visited the front desk and obtained the regular guest key to the room. Once again, after several tries, the door would not un-

Though it is somewhat difficult to see in this black and white, computer scanned reproduction, a bluish gray mist appeared hovering over the chair in this photograph. The white spot in the lower right hand corner, is the edge of Tim Pedersen's arm (in motion).

Joshua P. Warren (left) and Tim Pedersen (right) are shown standing on the fifth floor of the Main Inn. The strange orangish glow (circled) outside of 545, led to the original investigation of the hotel's most haunted room.

lock. We eventually had to have security come up and open the door. Even with all the rooms I stayed in, I never had that problem on any other occasion.

Once we were inside the room, we detected huge masses of fluctuating electromagnetic energy. With that, we immediately decided to return that same night with more equipment.

When we returned that night, greeted by the pale light of a full moon, we brought several ghost detecting instruments. These included a camera equipped to make infrared and ultraviolet photographs. This is made possible through the usage of special films and filters. However, it seemed that the energy in the room had quite drastically decreased, and whatever had been there before was there no longer. Aside from a window shutter mysteriously opening itself and then slamming shut, little else happened. Determined not to give up so easily, however, we decided to return the following night.

The next night I met with Mark-Ellis Bennett and Tim Vandenberghe shortly after midnight. We set up our equipment in 545. At one point, we set the electromagnetic field meter on the arm of a chair, and watched it patiently from a distance. For quite a while, it showed little or no reading. Then, suddenly, after a bit of observation, the meter began to detect a slight field. It grew stronger... and stronger... and stronger... and then began to fluctuate wildly. As Vandenberghe and I fired our cameras away, Bennett raced over to the sight and held out his hand. Bennett exclaimed that he felt a strange sensation on the surface of his skin. With that, Vandenberghe and I also rushed over. I held out my hand near Bennett's but, at first, felt nothing. However, just when Bennett

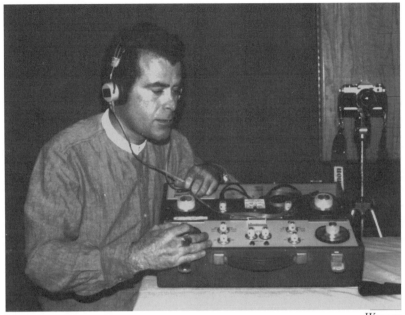

Warren

*Mark-Ellis Bennett is pictured here utilizing ultra-
and sub-sonic audio recording equipment.*

said he could no longer feel anything, I suddenly experienced a very bizarre sensation indeed.

An unexplainable feeling of weight pressed down on top of my hand, and the hair on my knuckles stood up. There was a force which felt thick and static-like against my skin. It felt neutral in temperature, however. Just as my mind was racing with thoughts, the feeling passed away from my hand. Only a few moments afterward, Vandenberghe, to my left, suddenly exclaimed, "I feel it!" A few seconds later, it passed away from his hand as well. Simultaneously, the reading on the meter dropped and disappeared. We each described experiencing the same sensations independently. It was as though some strange field had passed each of us on its way through the room. For the rest of the night, we received little energy readings from 545. By the end of the investigation, however, I would come to consider 545 the most haunted room in the Grove Park Inn.

Another night which proved to yield valuable results was January 20, 1996. That night I met with Tim Vandenberghe near midnight. At approximately 2:30 a.m., we set up a Van de Graff electrostatic generator in Elaine's. The device began dispersing ions and electrical discharges (blue sparks) of around four inches. Vandenberghe was observing the scenario through an infrared night vision scope. After approximately half an hour, the discharges from the machine began to grow significantly in size. They eventually reached a peak of over twelve inches long. The miniature lightning bolts then began to branch out in midair, as though being drawn to some invisible conductor. I made quite a few photographs as Vandenberghe continued to watch

Warren

*Tim Vandenberghe is shown peering through
his infrared night vision scope.*

through his scope, lying on his back and looking upwards. After this continued for a while, the activity then seemed to lessen in intensity.

After a period of lessened activity, I wandered into another part of the club. When I returned a few minutes later, Vandenberghe, his face pale and his eyes large, was standing on his feet. "I just saw something!" he exclaimed. Vandenberghe explained that he was lying on his back and watching the air above him with his naked eyes. Suddenly, seemingly coming from nowhere, a white streak of illumination passed across his range of vision and disappeared. We were eager to rule out a conventional cause for the event, and so we reproduced our actions that led to the occurrence. We watched carefully for reflections and light sources that may have simulated the sight. After two reproductions, we were still unable to recreate the effect. Even after searching the vacant lounge outside the club, we could find no natural explanation for what he claimed to have seen.

When I later developed the photographs from that night, I was amazed by what I saw. A photograph of the generator, made only ten minutes before the sighting, showed a white streak of illumination in the upper right-hand corner. The form apparently looks very similar to what Vandenberghe claims to have seen.

By the end of my field research, I had determined the two most "active" sites in the hotel were the fifth floor of the Main Inn (particularly Room 545) and Elaine's nightclub. By "active" I mean having the highest potential for producing a paranormal experience. This includes visual sightings of an apparition, audible indication, physical contact, or naturally unexplainable oc-

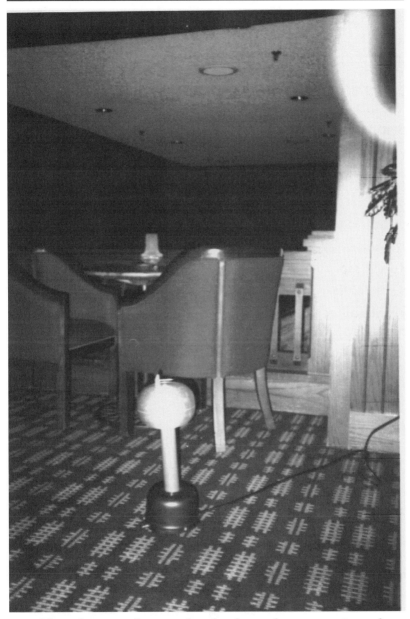

This photograph was taken by the author approximately ten minutes before Tim Vandenberghe claimed to see a "white streak" pass over his head. When developed, such a streak appeared in the top right hand corner of the picture. The photo was made with a 35mm camera using 1000 speed Kodak film.

currences. However, sightings and occurrences have been reported all over the hotel (especially the fourth floor of the Main Inn). Although, in these other areas of the hotel, energy fields may not exist in a constant stream of flux, energy levels instead come in occasional and sporadic bursts. I should also mention that Elaine's was not a part of the original Main Inn. It is therefore very mysterious that it should be home to so much supernatural activity.

Based upon my findings, I find it highly probable that if the Pink Lady did indeed exist and die so tragically, she stayed in Room 545. If she died from the legendary fall, I believe she fell outside of Room 545 and landed between Rooms 345 and 347. I should also note that, based upon my findings as well as eyewitness encounters, the paranormal occurrences most often take place in cold, dry months as opposed to warmer, more humid months. Best results are usually achieved near, or a few hours after, midnight.

During my investigation, results of the research were kept strictly confidential. This was to insure the utmost accuracy of the findings. Such delicate information can easily be contaminated. It was therefore gratifying when, after 545 had already been secretly located, we discovered first-hand paranormal experiences that had taken place there in years past.

Ernest Franks was a painter and foreman at the Grove Park Inn for over thirty years. He recalls having uncanny and uncomfortable sensations whenever he neared the room. "Chill bumps would come up on me when I'd have to go there," he said. Franks sensed these feelings as far back as the 1950s. He made it a point to

Warren

Room 545

be near 545 as little as possible, sending his men to work there instead.

In January of 1995, Kathleen Bennett, who presently works as the Engineering Facilities Manager at the hotel, had an unnerving experience near Room 545 as well. She was checking bathtubs in various rooms that had recently been reporcelained. As she approached 545 she'll never forget what happened. "I was going towards 545," she recalled. "I got about three or four feet away from it and, just all of a sudden—and it was *very* sudden—all of my hair stood on end. I had an extremely uncomfortable feeling... I got outta there *real* fast. I was very uncomfortable." Bennett then returned to her dispatch area and sent someone else to complete her task. Though Bennett said she is constantly traveling all over the hotel, that was the only time she ever had such an experience. Now, however, she steers clear of 545. "I'm not goin' back there," she said, "I was *that* uncomfortable."

Though some people, like Ernest Franks and Kathleen Bennett, describe uncomfortable sensations with their paranormal experiences, most people feel privileged to experience the supernatural. Although there are many reports of strange occurrences in the hotel, you must realize that, since 1913, millions of people must have passed through the timeless building. Others have worked at the hotel for many years and experienced absolutely nothing. To be graced by the presence of a spirit is, in its own way, an honor, indeed.

Despite my intense record searching and numerous interviews, the identity of the Pink Lady still remains a mystery. The hotel has virtually no records of past guests,

Vandenberghe

*Joshua P. Warren poses with a Wimshurst Generator.
This particular machine was designed by Charles Yost,
president of Dynamic Systems, Inc.*

and legal records from that bygone era are, supposedly, nonexistent. Who, then, was the Pink Lady?

Since there have been many strange reports from Rooms 441 and 443, which housed author F. Scott Fitzgerald during the summers of 1935 and 1936, for some it is a popular notion that she may be the ghost of Zelda Fitzgerald, his wife. Zelda, who was mentally unstable, died tragically in a fire at Highland Hospital. However, the facts behind Fitzgerald lend nothing to the lore that she may be the ghost. F. Scott died in California three years after staying at the Grove Park Inn, and Zelda died eight years after her husband. This would suggest that paranormal tales emanating from the rooms have nothing to do with Zelda Fitzgerald.

It should also be noted that there are some uncanny similarities between descriptions of the Pink Lady and descriptions of a phantom seen next door at the Battle Mansion (which now houses 13 WLOS TV). Could the same spirit be wandering both buildings? Decide for yourself after reading the next chapter.

SOMETHING IS GOING ON IN THE GROVE PARK INN. Call it phantoms. Call it madness. Call it what you will. But *something* is happening. Since, at least, the early 1940s, strange occurrences have livened up the stately halls of the ancient hotel at night.

They continue to see her— the elusive pink spectre that silently glides along the corridors. She comforts the children and bewilders the adults. She plays pranks on the employees, yet shies away from the curious. Who is she? Of what tragedy is she born? Regardless, though, of the pains she may have suffered in her past, surely it

April Boulware

From left to right, Joshua P. Warren, Tim Vandenberghe, and Mark-Ellis Bennett pose with some of the equipment used in the Pink Lady investigation.

must sometimes seem worth it now. Oh, but to wander in the Grove Park Inn throughout the decades... What stories she could tell! What celebrities she must have seen! What freedom she enjoys! A wall to us is a doorway to her.

The daily oddities that bewilder us so much are commonplace to the ghost. When we stand alone in a vacant hall, from where does the sudden burst of energy come that quickly dies away? What are these invisible fields that pass through empty rooms in the wee hours of morning? If not ghosts, then what? What are these strange images that appear in our photos? What has the film detected that we cannot always see?

The Grove Park Inn is more than a building. It is more than a hotel, or a resting place. It is a monument. It is the realization of one great man's dream. It is the legacy of a man who could have afforded any building on any site in the world. What he built, however, was *just right*.

To stand at a distance and look upon the great hotel is an experience all to itself. The monument, in all its power and glory, looks so mighty and strong—yet so natural it seems as though only God himself could have molded it. It has seen a thousand famous faces, and heard a thousand famous stories, yet the building is not impressed. For it is greater. Yet, in all its grandeur, it sits strong and silent, like a timeless mountain. "If only the walls could talk!" they say. But perhaps they can. Perhaps they do. They speak to the Pink Lady and perhaps, in her own way, the Pink Lady speaks to us.

To try to understand her is like trying to understand the Grove Park itself. It is deep and complex. We look upon the place and we know it is a mystery. A part of us tells us we shall never know all it secrets—yet we accept that. We accept it because it brings us such a feeling of warmth and comfort to simply walk through its doors. It brings us such peace and solitude that we allow it to be an enigma. It is older than we are—*wiser* than we are. Let it have its secrets.

Yes, the Pink Lady is real. Time and time again, she has deeply influenced those who are fortunate enough to see her. The nature of her existence we may never understand, but she is always out there... silently watching from a distance. It was Mark Twain who said, "Of course truth is stranger than fiction. *Fiction has to make sense.*" The legend of the Pink Lady has proven the value of his words once again.

Bennett

THE GHOST OF
13 WLOS TV

Nestled slightly below Macon Avenue, next door to the Grove Park Inn, channel 13 WLOS is one of the most highly regarded local news stations in the country. Each year, dozens come from across the nation to study its techniques and procedures. When news happens, they claim to be there first, but some say there is a story which even News 13 isn't quite sure how to tackle. Ironically enough, it hits closer to home than any other—their own building.

If there is an unusual occurrence in the building, anything from a door mysteriously closing itself to a piece of technical gadgetry defying the wishes of its operator, it's not uncommon to hear the mumble of the words "ghost" or "Alice," followed by a few lighthearted chuckles. But although many employees joke about the ghost in the three-story mansion, few feel comfortable being all alone in some of the more secluded areas of the building at night.

Bill Banner, Director of Retail Services, has worked at the station which bears the ominous number 13 for forty years. Although he has no fear of the spectre that supposedly roams the station, he has no doubt that it exists. "I've worked here two or three o'clock in the morning downstairs," Banner said, "when they had the laboratory down there. I would step out into the hall to come up the stairs and see the fleeting form of a woman. It was ghostly... you saw it, and then you didn't see it... all the way down at the end of the hall you would see this nebulous form. You'd look and it would just simply slide around the corner. You'd run down there and there was nothing there. Then you'd come to the bottom of the stairs and you could hear voices up here laughing and talking, and people walking and everything. So I would sneak up the stairs and go to the lobby, and you'd hear them going back and forth... I'd creep up the stairs, run up and look right fast—nothing there."

The woman that Banner speaks of is a chambermaid named *Alice*. According to popular legend, she fell, or was pushed, down a flight of steep, twisting steps in the corner of the mansion and broke her neck. Although no one knows when, or if, the incident occurred, Banner believes it may have taken place around the 1940s.

Bennett

Warren

Bill Banner

On another occasion, Bill Banner saw the phantom of Alice outside the building as well. He had been working until three in the morning, and went out on the lawn to take a break. Banner recalls the full moon shining brightly as he beheld the ghostly sight. "I saw this nebulous form of this woman in a purple gown... She just glided across the grass—there was no sound, whatsoever—and then down over the bank to the golf course. I dashed over there and looked and looked. There was nobody there." The golf course to which he refers adjoins the Grove Park Inn.

The stately News 13 mansion is actually a relatively prominent historical site. It is the previous home of Doctor Samuel Westray Battle. Battle, born in Nash County, North Carolina, in 1854, was a celebrated naval surgeon. After serving in the Navy for nearly ten years, he moved to Asheville, where he operated Oakland Heights, a tuberculosis sanitarium, along with another doctor, Paul Paquin. He was a popular and colorful figure known throughout the entire state, and among his many patients was Mrs. W. H. Vanderbilt, mother of George Vanderbilt. Although Battle enjoyed a favorable professional reputation, it was his social reputation for which he is best remembered. "He was a jolly ol' person," recalled Jane Bingham, a friend of the family. "Everybody *loved* Doctor Battle—he was a great wit."

It was not uncommon to see the boisterous Doctor Battle, toting a cape and cane, and sporting a curled handlebar mustache, strolling the streets of Asheville with an armload of flowers. Always a well groomed and polished gentlemen, he would hand a flower, with a bow, to each lady he encountered along his way (regardless

Joshua P. Warren

courtesy Asheville Citizen-Times

Dr. Samuel Westray Battle

71

of social class). It is easy to see how he became one of Asheville's most prominent and beloved personalities.

Doctor Battle died of a stroke April 29, 1927, the same year his mansion was built. It is therefore debatable as to whether the doctor, himself, spent any time in his new home. However, his widow (and second wife) Jane Hall Liddell continued to live in the mansion until her death in the early 1950s.

Although there were always servants in the home, there have been no records found to document a death like the one described in the legend. The servants did live on the third floor of the mansion, however, and ghost story proponents say that Alice resides largely in that section of the building. Friends of the family, including Jane Bingham, do not recall an unnatural death in the house. They do remember that the servants kept a very low profile, however.

It is interesting to note that Doctor Battle's first wife *was* named Alice. Alice Maude Belknap was the only daughter of Rear Admiral George E. Belknap. Alice Battle did indeed die an early death in Asheville on October 29, 1899, at age 36. An article in the *Asheville Daily Citizen*, dated the day after her demise, stated she died "at their home, 'Buncombe Lodge' after an illness of a year or more." The article went on to say, "Mrs. Battle was taken to Atlantic City for the summer, and while there was at first an improvement in her health, it did not continue and the family returned to Asheville, since which time the patient had gradually grown worse." The article never cited the specific cause of death, and that listing on her death certificate is, unfortunately, illegible. However, it may be assumed that she

Warren

*It is down these stairs that Alice is said to have
met her untimely demise.*

died of tuberculosis, which claimed many lives in such a manner during that era.

Alice Battle was well known and loved, just like her husband. However, Jane, the second Mrs. Battle, was generally not as popular. Though she threw large parties and enjoyed being the center of attention, many regarded her as being far less personable. It is said she was particularly disliked by the servants of the house, who missed Alice. If the classic legend of Alice is false, and she really was the doctor's first wife, some believe the ghost story was used to keep her memory alive. Among the servants, it was not acceptable to discuss Alice. A ghost story might, therefore, be used as a non-confrontational (and unchallengable) means of speaking about her.

After Jane Battle's death, the mansion was put up for sale. It was purchased in the early 1950s by Charles M. Britt, owner of WLOS Radio. Britt moved the station from downtown Asheville to the third floor of the mansion. He then decided to expand to television as well. On September 18, 1954, at 5:00 in the evening, WLOS Television made its debut. Britt continued to operate the radio station for years before it was sold.

It wasn't long after the station opened that rumors of supernatural activity began to drift about the building. Bob Caldwell, who has worked at the station for over thirty years, recalls several incidents when fellow employees experienced ghostly activity. "We had one radio announcer who was sitting at the console reading a piece of script, and his eyes were drawn over to the left. This girl's face was there, suspended, watching him. *And we lost one radio announcer because*

Warren / Pedersen

Alice?

of it."

The announcer to which Caldwell refers was a handicapped man who worked as a late night disk jockey. The announcer's console was on the third floor of the building, the area around which many of the sightings occur. One night, just before eleven o'clock, something quite unexpected happened. "He came down the stairs," recalled Caldwell, "and he wasn't coming down the stairs like a man crippled. He went out the door hurriedly, and never came back. He had seen it.

"We had a janitor here who saw it on the roof a couple of times, near the chimney," continued Caldwell. "A young lady in a long flowing gown. It's quite well known."

Caldwell said those who had encountered Alice over the years always gave a consistent description of the apparition. "She was a youngish girl—I understand she was in her twenties—in a long dress of the period... Most of them described it as a rather hazy, semi-opaque situation."

Bill Norwood worked at the television station for thirty years. To the public, he was best known as "Mr. Bill." Thousands of children in the Carolinas grew up watching his morning television show, featuring cartoons, entertainers, and fun activities. One morning, however, his show took a surprising turn into the realm of the unknown.

"I had an office in the extreme upper portion of the building," said Norwood. "One day, on my TV show, I had a witch come in from Morganton... This witch came on my TV show and did a seance, and tried to bring Elvis up from the dead, and all that stuff. I told her also about the ghost, Alice. But I didn't tell her until she and an apprentice witch were in my office.

"We were sitting there, and they were across from me, talking about doing the program. I said, 'By the way, there's supposed to be a ghost in this TV station, and the ghost is supposed to live on this floor.' The woman turned white—she just paled.

"She said, 'There is some mystic something in the air... I knew it! I knew there was someone here. She is in this building... I know it... I feel the sense of it.' She said, 'May I do a seance tonight?'

"So, at about midnight, we went upstairs in the attic and did a seance. She was supposed to have made contact with Alice. I don't know whether she did or not."

Norwood could not recall the specifics of what the witch said about Alice. He did remember, however, that she was primarily interested in whether Alice fell down the steps or was pushed.

Norwood also remembered a production member who claimed to see the spirit occasionally. "He swears that every once in a while he sees Alice in the window, looking out over Macon Avenue."

While investigating the mansion, the author and his colleagues found it considerably difficult to obtain any sort of scientific data regarding the activity. The vast array of computers and electrical equipment being utilized in the building makes obtaining accurate scientific readings almost impossible. There is without a doubt, however, an uncanny sense of dreariness about the place—especially late at night.

There are intriguing parallels between reports of seeing Alice, and reports of seeing the Pink Lady at the Grove Park Inn. In both cases, the apparition is that of a young woman. She is always wearing a long, old fashioned dress. The apparition is usually only glimpsed as she glides elusively throughout the building. In neither case has there ever been a report of any malicious activity. The persona of the spectre seems to be benevolent and somewhat melancholy.

There is only one outstanding difference between encounters in each place. At the Grove Park Inn, witnesses often mention the color pink when they see the ghost, while at the Battle Mansion there has been only one instance reported where a particular color was attributed to the apparition. This is in the case of Bill Banner, who described Alice's dress as appearing purple in the moonlight. Obviously, purple and pink can be quite similar colors, though, especially in different lighting conditions. It is also quite provocative that Banner claims ' he saw the ghost of Alice vanish onto the golf course which leads to the Grove Park Inn. Could the ghost of Alice and the Pink Lady be the same apparition? Does the spirit travel and spend time in both historical buildings?

The fact that both women supposedly died of a tragic fall makes the possibility even more compelling. There is also a version of the Pink Lady legend which states she was the wife of a doctor. This may be a direct allusion to the charming Doctor Battle.

If, indeed, the same spirit is wandering both locations, it makes the mystery of the ghost even more complex. Did the young lady die at the Battle Mansion or the Grove Park Inn? Was she a maid, a guest, or someone else?

In terms of documentation, it seems that it would be

Bennett

*This unusual gargoyle surveys the
grounds of the Battle Mansion.*

much easier to find evidence of death in the Battle Mansion rather than the Grove Park Inn. Obviously, a much more limited amount of people passed through the mansion. If a member of the residence died, then he or she would have been a member of the Asheville community. Chances are that local paperwork would have some mention of the death. It seems that family members might still exist in Asheville, as well. In the case of the Grove Park Inn, however, circumstances could have been very different. If the Pink Lady was a guest, then significant information of the death would likely be filed in the guest's hometown. If the media received no notification of the tragedy, then little permanent documentation would be left behind.

The archaic design of the Battle Mansion is stark, yet lavish at the same time. It appears distinguished and bold. In this respect, it contrasts somewhat with its timeless and rugged neighbor, the Grove Park Inn. However, though the place may have fewer stories to tell, it holds its own ground. And even though the two buildings appear so differently, there is still a strange balance between the two structures. To stand on the roof of the Battle Mansion and see the neighboring Grove Park Inn, or to do the opposite, is a peaceful and somewhat symmetrical experience. Though this balance may not be apparent at the surface of the two structures, it seems instead to rest somewhere just below the surface. It is on an enigmatic and surreal level that the two monuments seem to be joined. Perhaps it is on this plane, a level beyond our understanding, that a lost spirit wanders between the two for eternity.

Warren

THE CEMETERY AT ERWIN HIGH SCHOOL

N o one really knew how long the cemetery across the road from the Old County Home on Lee's Creek Road had been there. It rested atop a desolate hill beside the old Erwin High School (presently Erwin Middle School). Many believed the ancient bone yard began as a family cemetery in the late 1700s, but the only marked tombstone in the field bore the inscription:

In Memory Of
Charlotte K.
Wife of
J.N. Snelson
Born Sept. 30th, 1856
Died May 3rd, 1883

County officials of the time had no idea how many bodies were buried in the lonely field. Little did they know that their original estimate of 200 would skyrocket to over 1,000. Only 73 accounts were ever recorded, and the explanation is a simple one: Few really cared.

The cemetery was one for those in society that most people felt were best forgotten. It was a pauper's cemetery, owned by the county, which was the final resting place for criminals, vagabonds, beggars, forgotten elders and all poor and underprivileged residents of Buncombe. Billy Pritchard, an *Asheville Citizen-Times* writer, said it best in a 1973 article:

> *They were lonely, unwanted and forgotten souls alive, and no one shed any tears over their pauper's graves when they left this world as all men do, with nothing. But they had nothing in life either, and when their souls were taken away, it must have been for them a better place. In most cases, there were no flowers, no songs of praise, no funeral procession, no last words of prayer over the cheap wooden coffin and no tombstone to mark their passing. They were no more thought of under the ground than they had been above it. Hidden away in rest homes, mental hospitals and jails where they eventually died, these souls were wards of the state and county welfare department. If anyone loved them at all, it was these institutions which kept them alive and afforded their burials at death.*

The bodies of these melancholy souls were hurriedly and carelessly buried in most cases. There was usually no embalming or funeral services, and many corpses were simply wrapped in a sheet and shallowly buried to save a bit of time as well as the taxpayer's money. There was no marking of bodies in most cases, and many times one assigned the duty of burying a body would dig up another in the process. Because of this, many were bur-

Bennett

*It is this benevolent hill that held the
greatest concentration of bodies.*

ied coffin-on-coffin and, in other incidents, there were cases of mass graves.

The lonely place was referred to by most locals simply as "potter's field," but many others called it County Home Graveyard. The County Home controlled the usage of the graveyard, and although it's uncertain how long bodies had been buried there, it began using the field as a pauper's cemetery around 1905.

For an overwhelming amount of time, the neglected souls had rested in the damp, dismal earth undisturbed— a span of time which ended in 1973.

It was in that year the Buncombe County School Board decided to build a new Erwin High School on the property the cemetery then occupied. The decision was immediately met by opposition from several county officials and many private citizens. R. Curtis Ratcliff, then chairman of the Buncombe County Board of Commissioners, was particularly concerned with the proposed $64,000 of taxpayers' money that would be invested in the project. Democrat member Roy Trantham said he would never vote public funds for moving dead people. "I think they ought to be left alone," he said.

One concerned citizen, Mrs. Lula Edens of Asheville, insisted that a marker be placed on the grounds to commemorate the dead. "I'll never die happy until I know there's something up there. I was horrified when I learned that potter's field was unmarked. I have suggested one large, marble marker with an Old Rugged Cross on top of it, and an inscription that reads, 'Those Names Known Only To God—Peace Be Unto You.'" Mrs. Edens never received her wish, however, and the school board decided to begin excavation of the grounds.

Bennett

Phillip Ellen Contractors, Inc., of Southern Pines, North Carolina, was hired to take care of the job. The team of seven men, using only shovels, mattocks and a bulldozer (which they were only allowed to use to cover up the graves) began working for the fee of $79 a grave. Their only method of locating the bodies was by plunging a T-handled steel rod into the dirt, feeling for soft spots. For added assistance, some Erwin High students were hired to help locate the graves for a few dollars a body. After working in the field for a while, the estimate of 200 bodies quickly jumped to 400, then 800, and finally to over 1,000.

The grounds were a confusing mass of jumbled and nameless remains. Most of the unknown corpses were severely decomposed, and dumped into small wooden boxes for transport. Many anonymous observers claimed there was very little care taken in the excavation, and bodies were laid in rows in the open, despite potential health hazards to the teachers and students who were occasionally allowed to visit the site.

One teacher (who requested anonymity) vividly recalled a disturbing sight. Upon visiting the scene for observation, she remembered the opening of a particular coffin. Inside was the skeleton of an apparently young woman. There were remnants of an ancient, worn gown on the pale bones, and long red hair flowed from the skull. Cradled in her arms was the tiny skeleton of a baby. One might assume the two had died together in childbirth.

R. Curtis Ratcliff visibly shivered while recalling a gruesome sight he witnessed while visiting the excavation. "They punched a hole in a coffin and reached down in there and drug out a skull and threw it over on the ground. Some false teeth fell out...the hair fell off."

Bennett

The photographer noted that some areas of the hill
contained strange sunken spots. The dark spots in the
above photograph show two such depressions.

Some bones were so carelessly strewn around that there were several incidents where students played practical jokes with the human remains. One morning, residents of the area awoke to find skulls mounted on various fence posts around the community.

Phillip Ellen paid his workers $3 an hour or $12 a grave for every one over four that was found, excavated, and approved—having been found with remains inside. The particular operation was so gruesome that it was the last job for some crew members who dug up the cemetery. One member of the crew, Steve Belcher, had followed Ellen all over the country digging up graves—a job he said didn't bother him until he started working on Potter's Field. In an interview, Belcher recollected, "We were digging on the other side of the field and struck one that was still intact. I got sick. I mean, it really bothered me."

The bodies located were placed into pine boxes of three different sizes. The most often used was a box 36 inches long, 8 inches wide and a foot deep. More substantial remains were placed in boxes 5 feet and 6 feet long. Ellen once remarked, "Actually, the boxes we're putting them in are better than the ones that they were buried in originally."

In a few weeks, the firm had completed the excavation, supposedly having removed nearly a thousand bodies. They were reburied on a quiet hill behind what is presently West Buncombe Elementary School. However, according to an *Asheville Citizen-Times* article published October 30, 1973, Fred H. Martin, Superintendent at the time, stated that an estimated 250 to 300 of the bodies speculated to be there *would not*

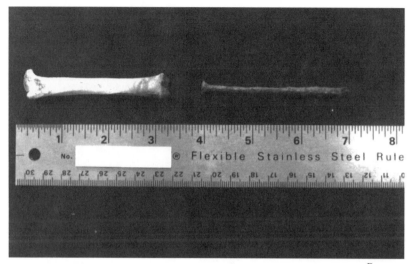

Bennett

While on the hill, the photographer found the above bone and old nail. The origin of both items remains unidentified.

be moved.

The new Erwin High School was built directly beside the small hill which held the main concentration of bodies. The mound is now a benevolent barrier between the school and the football stadium. Many say, however, that unmarked graves of the antiquated cemetery are strewn all about the property, and there are even invalidated tales that, in time, bones have actually worked their way up through the soil occasionally. Whether such claims are true or not, no one really knows for sure. They, like the cemetery, remain a great source of mystery and speculation.

It is not uncommon to hear tales of strange phenomena that surround the school. Janitors reluctantly pass along rumors about eerie noises and footsteps that can be heard within the vacant halls late at night, long after the hustle and bustle of the school day. Some have even suggested, with a trifle of humor, that the dishonored spirits cursed the neighboring stadium and football team. From 1991 to 1995, Erwin's varsity team had 33 consecutive losses, earning a losing state record and approaching a national one.

Obviously, no one will say for sure whether or not the grounds of Clyde A. Erwin High School are haunted. Death is a sensitive subject, and those who have stories to tell are reluctant to publicize them. Perhaps many at the school find comfort in trying to forget the massive ocean of decaying corpses that once surrounded the grounds. Such a morbid notion is sometimes best when repressed to the back of the mind. It seems, though, that if ever a place had reason to be haunted, these would be prime conditions. If the macabre orgy of pitiful souls never found true peace and justice while in the world of the living, perhaps they dwell restlessly in the afterworld.

What the ground beneath Erwin High School now holds is perhaps known best by those who have already departed us in time. Whether or not students tread each day over the remains of bodies is a mystery. But regardless of what Erwin's soil may hide today, the essence of what was once there shall live forever. Bob Terrell sums it up best with a statement about the grounds, before the excavation, from a *Citizen-Times* article:

> *It's a beautiful hilltop, fringed by a handful of proud, old oaks and backed by a long row of mimosa trees. Leafless now, the gnarled branches of the mimosas reach skyward like so many souls lost in a wilderness. But it is no wilderness. The view from the hilltop, over a rickety board fence that separates the tract from fields below, is one of rolling pastureland and thick forests, of farm buildings and homes, and life itself. Why, then, such an eerie feeling? Why does one feel so desolate standing there with the north wind laying icy hands upon his shoulders? It is not the wind that sends a chill up one's spine. It is the simple knowledge that this is a cemetery.*

Bennett

MURDER IN THE BATTERY PARK HOTEL

It was the morning of July 17, 1936, that W. L. Clevenger, a guest at the Battery Park Hotel, approached his niece's room to awaken her for breakfast. Her name was Helen Clevenger. The blonde nineteen-year-old New York University honor student had been visiting her uncle, a professor at North Carolina State University, over her summer break. The two had been staying in the historic Battery Park Hotel during their visit to Asheville. The trip had been wonderful so far—but all that was about to horribly change.

As W. L. Clevenger approached Room 224, he could never have prepared himself for the sight that awaited him on the other side of the door. He knocked a few times, and paused. No response. He knocked again. Still no response. At that point, Mr. Clevenger twisted the doorknob a bit, and it turned easily—unlocked. The perplexed man slightly cracked the door, and then disappeared inside. A few moments later, he stepped back into the doorway. Tears were streaming down his flushed face. A hotel carpenter, working on a corridor near the girl's room, looked to him with bewilderment. With that, Mr. Clevenger's face twisted into a painful frown. A sickening whimper escaped from deep in his throat, *"Come—look what they've done to her."* The carpenter, as well as other hotel employees, rushed to the room.

However, they too were just as shocked to be greeted by the macabre scene.

In the midst of the rainy, dreary night, Helen Clevenger had been brutally murdered. She lay on her back in a pool of thick blood. Her feet, and the lower portion of her legs, were crumpled under her body. It appeared as though she had been on her knees, begging for her young life, when the merciless killer delivered the final blow. Immediately, the authorities were called, and their discoveries illustrated, even more so, the ruthlessness of the murderer.

Helen had been savagely beaten. Her beautiful, delicate face had been viciously slashed to pieces with a sharp instrument. One of the blows had been delivered with such force that it penetrated her face, just below the left eye, and protruded through the roof of her mouth. There was a bullet hole in the upper left portion of her chest. Her green striped pajamas were drenched in blood from the wound. Flesh around the bullet hole was burned by gunpowder, indicating the muzzle of the gun had been pressed against her body, presumably to muffle the sound of the shot.

In his autopsy report, the county coroner said the bullet penetrated the upper portion of the left lung. It stopped under the skin of the girl's back, slightly under her left shoulder blade. The wound caused major hemorrhaging, and Helen probably died within a matter of minutes. The coroner reported the bullet as being slightly smaller than a .32 caliber. However, he was unable to positively identify the sharp weapon which was used to slash her face. In the early stages of the investigation, the police would come to believe it was a can opener.

The coroner estimated the time of death to be around one o'clock in the morning.

But why? What was the motive for such a heinous crime? Never before had anyone felt threatened sleeping within the stately walls of The Battery Park Hotel. Such famous people as Dorothea Dix, Babe Ruth, Lou Gehrig, Ward Bond, Grace Kelly, Susan Hayward, Van Heflin, Boris Karloff, Robert Mitchum, and Mickey Rooney had settled into peaceful slumber within the old hotel. Hordes of governors and congressmen had passed through routinely. So why now? What had this innocent young woman done to warrant such an attack? Robbery as a motive was quickly dismissed by the authorities. Twelve dollars was found in Helen's pocketbook, and a wrist watch lay on a chair near the bed. Nothing had been taken from the room. Why then would a hotel guest, a complete stranger, be so brutally beaten and murdered?

There was one question, however, that authorities sought to answer more than anything—*who?* Who would perpetrate such a disgustingly horrific act? Initially, the only significant clues came from Durham Jones, an African-American hall boy.

Jones was in the bellhop's service room on the south end of the hotel lobby. The lobby was desolate and dark, with the exception of occasional flashes of lightning illuminating the window panes. The light was turned on in the service room as Jones leisurely sipped a glass of lemonade. Since only the service room light was turned on, it was a bit difficult to discern details of motion in the dark halls outside. However, around one in the morning, Jones glimpsed a man as he dashed into the office of Pat M. Branch, the hotel manager. With that, Jones quietly stepped into the lobby and approached the manager's office. Eager to get a look at the mysterious figure, he crouched behind a desk in the office. Seeing no one, Jones started back into the lobby, heading toward another bellboy. Suddenly, he heard the screen door slam between the manager's office and the hotel porch.

Jones immediately rushed to the hotel's main door. Looking up, he saw a figure vault from the porch railing onto the wet street. The elusive figure ran to O. Henry Avenue, continued toward Haywood Street, and then disappeared into the dreary night.

Durham Jones was unable to give a good description of the figure he had seen that night. He said it appeared to be a man weighing 160 or more pounds. Jones estimated the man to be five feet and eight or nine inches tall. He also noted that the man wore no hat.

Immediately, a massive manhunt was executed in Asheville. A gruesome murder, the likes of this one, was unheard of in this peaceful mountain town. In the weeks after the Clevenger murder, a number of Asheville citizens were questioned and even taken into custody. Time and time again, the police were given false hope by dead ending leads. Newspapers chronicled developments in the case daily, and the public anxiously followed the progress of the investigation. The case was so sensational that it gained a great deal of national attention. At one point, the *New York Mirror* published a double-page spread of photographs and highlights from the investigation.

On August 9, 1936, the persistence of law enforcement officials paid off. A 22-year-old black hall boy, Martin Moore, confessed to the crime. The murderer had been a hotel employee the entire time.

When interrogated about the murder, Moore, a native of Spartanburg, South Carolina, claimed that he had not intended to kill Clevenger. He said that he had planned to rob someone. Moore claimed that he had first gone to Room 218 and turned the handle. However, the room was locked. He then supposedly tried Room 219, and found it locked as well. When he turned the handle of 224, though, the door opened. With that, Moore quietly entered the room.

When Moore stepped into the room, he claimed that Clevenger raised from her bed, startled. Bewildered, she asked him what he wanted. Moore said he told her he thought the room was unoccupied. Clevenger told him to leave at once or she would call the office. He claimed that Clevenger then rose from the bed and approached him. With that, Moore produced a .32 caliber pistol. Oddly designed, there was a jagged piece of metal that protruded from the butt of the gun. When Clevenger saw the gun, she began to scream hysterically. Moore forced the pistol against her torso and fired. As she crumpled to the ground, he beat her face with the butt of the gun. The protruding piece of metal had slashed deep into her soft complexion.

In a panic, Moore had then rushed through the building and jumped from the mezzanine, as Durham Jones had seen him. He vanished into the rainy night. Only a few hours later, however, he reported to work as usual. Moore calmly worked his shift as though it was just another night on the job.

Though Martin Moore's account of what happened in the room was the only one police had, they did not believe his tale. They felt sure that Moore had specifically entered the room of Helen Clevenger to "criminally assault" her. For them, robbery seemed an unlikely motive.

There was obviously an uproar from the public. A black man had confessed to murdering a white girl in cold blood. The year was 1936. His fate was sealed. Martin Moore died in the gas chamber for his unspeakable crime.

THE BATTERY PARK HOTEL WHICH SET THE SCENE for the Clevenger murder was actually the *new* Battery Park Hotel. The original hotel was completed in 1886. Its construction was commissioned by Colonel Franklin Coxe, a native of Rutherford County. The original structure and grounds, almost palace-like in appearance, covered nearly 25 acres on a huge hill overlooking Asheville. Once completed, the hotel, perhaps the finest in Western North Carolina, was a great social center in Asheville. It was visited by travelers from all across Victorian era America. In 1921, however, the hotel was purchased by E.W. Grove. Grove wanted to modernize downtown Asheville to make it more suitable as a thriving business center. He planned to tear down the old hotel and build a new one in its place. Across from it, he wanted to construct a magnificent indoor arcade. His creation is now known as the Grove Arcade.

Grove's job of constructing a new hotel was a mighty one indeed. He wanted the ground on which the hotel rested to be flat. Therefore, after demolishing the old hotel, he hired crews to painstakingly dig away the hill on which it had been built. The massive loads of dirt were then transported to a large ravine nearby. Once the ravine

courtesy the Ewart M. Ball Collection, Ramsey Library, UNC-Asheville

*The old Battery Park Hotel seemed like a palace
overlooking the city below.*

was filled in, it became what is presently Coxe Avenue.

The new Battery Park Hotel, a highrise brick structure, officially opened its doors to tourists in 1924. Though far less elaborate than its predecessor, it captured Grove's feel for the "modern era." Grove was proud of the hotel, one of his last contributions to Asheville. For Grove himself died in his new Battery Park Hotel on January 27, 1927.

Who would have guessed that, less than a decade after the great builder's own death in the hotel, it would be the site of one of Asheville's greatest crimes? Unfortunately, the murder of Helen Clevenger was not the last of the tragedies to surround the great hotel. As the years passed, more scenes of unnatural death seemed to be drawn to the site—particularly suicides.

At 7:30 a.m. on September 2, 1943, Clifton Alheit, aged 46, jumped 150 feet to his death from the top of the hotel. Alheit pulled a chair up to the guard rail to facilitate his jump.

Again, in 1972, another man jumped from the roof of the hotel. Michael J. Byrnes, aged 28, was a patient at Highland Hospital. Byrnes was supposedly going to attend Sunday morning mass at Basilica of St. Lawrence (then St. Lawrence Catholic Church). After exiting a taxi, the man went instead to a freight elevator located in the rear of the hotel, and used it to ascend to the top. Byrnes, too, used a chair to get over a guard rail, and then executed his final plunge.

In the cases of both men, no suicide notes were left, and there were no witnesses to their deaths. It seems a bit uncanny that each suicide was similar to the other.

The Battery Park Hotel now serves as an apartment

complex for senior citizens. Access to the hotel is strictly guarded—especially to the roof. Though traffic through the building is nothing compared to its illustrious past, there are chilling stories that still manage to seep to the world outside.

It is said that the spirit of Helen Clevenger has been seen in the hotel. On stormy nights, she is sometimes glimpsed wandering through the halls. She can be seen especially when the hallways are dark, and a flash of blue lightning illuminates the window panes—just as it did the night she was brutally murdered. Though the rooms have now been renumbered, the resident of what was once 224 may have some interesting stories to tell, for certain. There are some anonymous claims that, at one o'clock in the morning, on the anniversary of the murder, a blood-red haze surrounds the window of her cursed room. But who is brave enough to venture there that time of night?

It is also interesting to note that the young girl's name was Helen. Some believe it was her name that may have been given to the ghost on Beaucatcher Mountain (which you'll read about later).

It is also quite commonplace to hear tales from by-standers who inadvertently catch a glimpse of some-thing falling from the roof of the Battery Park Hotel. When they search for the source of the vision, however, there is nothing to be found. Could they be seeing the replay of a suicide? Does such a tragic event somehow embed itself permanently in the environment? Who knows?

For some reason, the new construction of E.W. Grove seems to harbor a sense of death. The tall, unflinching building does seem a bit ominous in the backdrop of the city. Perhaps it is a mere coincidence that these deaths, and more, have occurred at the hotel. Surely, to some, it may seem a bit rash to jump to a superstitious conclusion. But, then again, there is one last detail that the author has neglected to share. Coincidence? Perhaps. But how strange it is to find that the Battery Park Hotel is nothing other than *thirteen* stories tall.

Bennett

THE REED HOUSE

Imagine, if you will, the classic haunted house. If you found it, what would you expect to see? Chances are, it would be a large, old, wooden mansion of several floors. You would find it sitting atop a hill, looming down from its ancient perch. The roof would rise in a series of points and intriguing angles. Countless windows would surround its sides, looking out like a thousand leering eyes to view the wooded grounds. Steps at the front of the house would lead up to a large, spacious porch, and then to a massive door, where a tarnished bell awaits the ringing of a mortal hand.

If you made it through that door, the first thing you would expect to see is a long, steep, dark staircase, leading up to a maze of vast rooms, filled with priceless antiquities. If you walked up that staircase, you would be greeted midway by a large, dismal portrait with eerie eyes. As you passed it, you might feel the staring eyes boring into your back, its pupils following your ascent to the rooms. And above the rooms, of course, would rest a dusty attic, a dark place for all the spirits to hide until the sun goes down.

There would be a hardwood floor, high ceilings, a billiard room, and precarious lighting which played with the shadows near every corner. It might be easy to get lost in the unusual design of the halls and stairways—

especially by candle light, when there is no electricity, and the melancholy abode seems to welcome the lightning from a brewing storm outside. Then again, a frightful journey through the house might be shortened by use of a secret passage concealed in an ordinary wall. But then, who knows what spooks may linger there?

Next, of course, you might want to imagine what sights and sounds would await you as the witching hour approached. But no—stop. Why imagine when I can tell you? That's right, there's no need to imagine any more, because that house is real. It sits atop a large hill near Biltmore Village. The Victorian mansion that carries all these wonderful traits, and more, is a bed and breakfast called the Reed House.

The house was built in 1892 by Samuel Harrison Reed. Reed, born in Swannanoa on May 6, 1851, was the senior partner of Reed & Van Winkle, a highly esteemed law firm in Asheville. He is best remembered as an attorney for George Vanderbilt. Though he was a very wealthy man, he was never greedy or selfish. Those of the public both loved and respected him. He was considered a very trustworthy and reliable man, unlike, of course, the stereotypical lawyer.

On June 18, 1873, he married Miss Jessie Wingate, the only daughter of Thomas Wingate, a prominent citizen of Asheville. The Reeds produced nine children. However, quite tragically, only four of them lived to adulthood.

When Samuel Reed built his large house, the hill it sat atop, now covered with homes, was somewhat desolate. The 18-acre tract was called Reed's Hill. The impressive mansion was quite a spectacle showcased atop

courtesy Marge Turcot

Samuel Reed

the mound, very suitable for a man of Reed's prestige. Complete with 62 windows, 10 fireplaces, and running water from a windmill and gravity system in the back, it was a model of luxury. But obviously, the house is most famous for the trademark turret exquisitely positioned between its two wings. Reed, the owner of thousands of acres, sold land below the house to George Vanderbilt for what is now Biltmore Village.

Samuel Reed's life must have been filled with a good deal of sadness. After losing five of their children, his wife died in 1904. Only six months later, in 1905, the good lawyer himself followed. Both he and his wife were in their early fifties. They were buried in Riverside Cemetery.

The Reeds' four teenage children were sent to live with relatives. After being rented out for years, the mansion was eventually sold to a developer around 1915. From that time on, it continued to change hands throughout the decades. At one point, during the 1940s, it was divided into apartments, and shared by four families for many years. Having been mistreated through time, the Reed House sat abandoned for eight years during the 1960s and early 1970s. It was in 1972, however, that it first caught the eye of Marge Turcot.

Mrs. Turcot, a nurse at St. Joseph's Hospital, as well as the President of the Preservation Society of Asheville and Buncombe County, immediately saw the potential for renovating the historical old mansion. City inspectors had already begun condemnation proceedings when Turcot and her husband purchased the house in May of 1973. Upon moving from their home on Sunset Mountain, Turcot and her family knew they had their work

courtesy Marge Turcot

Jessie Reed shortly before her death

cut out for them. The renovation process was painstaking, but swift repairs and restorations had to be made. On the very first night the family stayed in the mansion, however, they experienced a strange occurrence.

"Our first night, no beds had been set up," recalled Turcot, "so we had to sleep on the dining room floor. Dog tired as we were, we were awakened around midnight by the sound of heavy boots on the back stairs. Any mother with a teenage daughter knows what that means: an unauthorized male visitor. About ten minutes later, I crept upstairs, ready for a family 'council,' and peeked into her room. She was asleep—and alone. So were my sons. Everyone was asleep.

"For several years thereafter, every time someone new slept in the house for the first time, we would hear those same boots on the back steps, just about midnight. Our friendly ghost was checking them out."

That first night was only a preview of the unexplainable occurrences that would take place throughout the house. One of the prominent supernatural recurrences would take place in the billiard room. Time and time again, Turcot would hear the the rack break on the pool table. Then the balls would strike each other as though a regular game were being played. Thinking that, perhaps, some of her children were playing pool, Turcot was always amazed to find the room had been vacant the entire time. "My personal hunch," added Turcot, "is that it is Samuel Reed playing pool."

On one occasion, a ball completely disappeared from the table. "We tore the house apart looking for it," said Turcot. There was no trace of the ball for several weeks. However, upon returning home from a Bele Chere booth

Bennett

*It is this pool table where a spectral game is sometimes played.
Note: This is an infrared photograph.
Since it does not detect visible light, all but
one of the balls appears solid white.*

one afternoon, she found the lost ball sitting in the empty space in the rack. To this day, Turcot, a woman of science, is bewildered by that event. "We never believed the stuff, you know," she said of her and her husband's original views on the supernatural. "Any time anybody talked about this stuff I used to always listen respectfully, but in my head I was thinking, *'uh huh.'* However, now I believe."

Turcot's children would often experience strange phenomena in the house as well. Aside from hearing pool games in the middle of the night, they would observe bedroom doors opening and closing when no one else was around.

When the outside lights were originally installed in the house, the family could not get them to work. Even an electrician Turcot called failed to get them operational. However, one night, upon returning to the empty house from dinner, all the lights were "blazing." Since then, they have functioned completely normally.

Turcot's renovations gave the mansion a whole new life. The house that was once almost condemned is now listed in the National Register of Historic Places, and the interior and exterior have been declared a local historic property by the Historic Resources Commission. Turcot opened the Reed House as a bed and breakfast in 1985. Since then, the house has seen guests from all over the world. Guests at the Reed House love the comfort and authentic environment of the settings, even though they themselves commonly observe paranormal occurrences.

Guests have experienced everything from lights mysteriously turning on and off and books falling off shelves

courtesy Marge Turcot

*This is believed to be the wedding photograph
of Mr. and Mrs. Reed*

121

to presences in their rooms at night. One woman staying at the bed and breakfast was awakened several times during the night by her shower turning on again and again. Guests may also sometimes hear the sounds of children playing around the house, although Turcot's children are now adults, living in various parts of the country. The sounds of heavy feet walking about the house, as well as unexplainable noises from the attic, abound.

One night, a young couple was playing pool in the haunted billiard room. The skeptical man was badgering his wife about her belief in ghosts. "Aw, you don't really believe in ghosts, do you?" he said with a smirk. Just as the words escaped his lips, an old folded up curtain fell from the top of a bookcase and landed at his feet.

In the summer of 1995, Turcot's teenage nephew was sleeping in one of the upstairs rooms alone. He claimed the next morning that, during the middle of the night, he had perceived a "presence" walking around his bed. Though certain of what he had experienced, he could not see anyone in the room.

The following night, two guests were staying in that same room. The next morning, one of the guests, a woman, claimed that she too had sensed a presence walking about the room (though she had no knowledge of the previous night's experience). Although she could not see anyone either, she claimed that she intuitively sensed some information about the presence. She said it was a female, and that her name was "Thelma." Despite research, Turcot has never found anyone previously associated with the mansion by this name. However, activities that took place in the house throughout the years are largely an enigma. Turcot, and her sister, have also claimed to have sensed such a presence wandering about the house.

In a place where such ghostly activity is so plentiful, you may think that guests would be scared away. However, it is just the opposite. Turcot believes the haunting of the house is an added attraction. As a matter of fact, many guests come to the house with the sole intention of experiencing supernatural occurrences. Since activities have always been benign, Turcot believes there is nothing to fear. "We ignore things now," says Turcot, being so accustomed to the continuing activity. For her, such strange activity is a part of everyday living. "I don't even remember all the things that have happened over the years," she says. "It's never been scary, it's just beyond our understanding."

The origin of the ghost (or ghosts) in the house is something of a mystery. Although there is no conclusive record, it is assumed that Samuel Reed, his wife, and his five young children all died in the house. If this is the case, and all of their spirits still haunt the abode, this could explain most all of the activity. Perhaps the heavy boots and pool playing is Mr. Reed, the female presence is Mrs. Reed, and the children heard playing around the house are the spirits of the children who tragically died. But then, if Samuel Reed is playing pool, with whom is he playing? He was known to sometimes play a game with George Vanderbilt in life. Is it possible that Vanderbilt himself sometimes visits the home today for a ghostly game of pool?

The Reed House is a living legend. It is a ghost story come to life, or a Hollywood set lost in the mountains. Even on a bright, sunny day, there is something gloomy about the place looming down over you. Its mammoth wooden door contains more than a century of stories, experiences, and, as it seems, souls. It is the archetypal spooky old house, yet at the same time it is a luxurious antiquity. Places like the Reed House remind us of what life was truly like in the bygone glory of Asheville's most famous era. It retains a legacy of such old-fashioned enchantment that, once one steps through the door, he or she does not desire to leave for a very long time— *just ask Samuel Reed.*

The Reed House
119 Dodge Street
Asheville, NC 28803
(828) 274-1604

The Reed House is open for guests
from May 1 to November 1.

Pedersen

HELEN'S BRIDGE AND ZEALANDIA

If you travel up Beaucatcher Mountain, along the winding path of Vance Gap Road, soon you will round a sharp bend to find the road enclosed by a narrow canyon. And at the top of the ancient ravine, you will discover the remains of a decrepit, rickety bridge. Its weathered beams and roughly hewn stones support decades of tangled vines and undergrowth. It has silently rested above the roadway for so long that it has burrowed its way into the natural surroundings—so much, in fact, that it's hard to imagine a time when the bridge was not there. It is a peaceful sight, and yet there is something so dark and melancholy which surrounds it. It is a sight which one glances when, almost immediately, a voice seems to whisper somewhere in the background, *"this place has a story to tell."* And so it does.

This is the infamous Helen's Bridge, a name which has lingered in the minds of most locals for longer than they can remember. For generations, there have been stories of a haunting which surrounds the bridge, as well as the nearby castle, Zealandia. As with most legends of the sort, there are several versions of the "true" story, each one with its own twists and variations of the circumstances. The most popular version captures the true persona of the bridge itself, however, with a dark and dismal mixture of tragedy and despair.

It is said that in the late nineteenth or early twentieth century, a woman, Helen, and her beloved daughter lived in a humble house on the mountain. Helen, a quiet and God-fearing woman, cared for nothing in the world more than her only child. Tragedy struck one night, however, when the daughter, at an unknown age, was playing in Zealandia and one of the rooms caught fire. Since most of the castle is relatively fireproof, the blaze consumed only one room. However, Helen's precious daughter was trapped in the inferno, and burned to death. One may easily imagine the darkness that engulfed Helen's soul when she was told of her daughter's untimely demise. Her whole world destroyed in the blaze, the distraught woman walked onto the desolate bridge under the veil of nightfall. She tied a noose to the side of the ominous structure and, in one final burst of despair, hanged herself above the roadway.

The next morning, the residents of the community awoke to find Helen, in her long, old-fashioned dress, swinging and swaying back and forth from the creaky rafters of the bridge. It is not difficult to imagine the disturbing image of such a grisly scene.

Since that fateful morning, countless numbers of people claim to have seen the apparition of Helen wandering about the mountainside and adjacent castle. She mournfully seeks the spirit of her long-lost daughter. It is an especially popular notion for local adolescents to stop their cars under the bridge on a foggy, moonlit night and call, "Helen, come forth... Helen, come forth... Helen, come forth." On the third call, it is said the spectre will sometimes appear. According to some accounts, if she touches the vehicle, a permanent hand print will be implanted in the finish of the paint.

One story surrounding the bridge recounts the experience of a man driving alone, late at night, down the mountain. After passing under the bridge (headed toward Tunnel Road) and rounding the sharp curve, he looked over to find a woman walking up the side of the embankment. He instinctively stopped his vehicle, sensing that perhaps an accident had taken place and that the woman's car had gone over the side. Rolling down his window, he was approached by the woman, who looked dismally out of place. She wore a long, white dress. Her complexion was pale, and her face bore a blank expression. There was an uncanny emptiness about her as she quietly drew closer to the car. "Can I help you?" the man called out. "Do I need to call an ambulance?" But the woman's face showed no signs of reaction to his inquiries. She simply stared penetratingly into his eyes, and when her mouth parted, an eerie voice escaped.

"Have you seen my daughter?"

It was then, for the first time, that the legend of Helen resurfaced in his mind. Long before he had heard the ghost story, and dismissed it as just that. But now the image of the lifeless woman stood before him, waiting for his answer to her phenomenal question.

His dry throat almost choked on the "No" he scarcely managed to reply. With that, he could sense the spirit's mood turn even bleaker. She took a few delicate steps backwards, and then began to softly glide, fading away into the darkness.

Immediately, in panic, the man hit the accelerator. His car screeched as it barely held the pavement on each turn of the perilous road. It was the last time he ever ventured near Helen's Bridge after dark.

Aside from hearsay, there is little proof of the circumstances supporting the legend. Records, as scant as they are, have never been found that prove a direct link between fact and fiction. It can be easily assumed, however, that any historic link which may have given rise to the legend might be found within the majestic walls of Zealandia. There is even a version of the legend which speculates that Helen was a mistress of one of the castle's owners, and when she became pregnant with the owner's illegitimate child, she was rejected by her lover. In deep depression, she then proceeded to hang herself from the rafters of the bridge. A story of this secretive nature would be even more difficult to prove, however. Besides, since its completed construction in 1889, the castle has seen a number of owners. It's hard to say which ones may have contributed to the legend of Helen.

Zealandia, nestled in the woods a short distance from the bridge, was built by John Evans Brown, a native of Pennsylvania. From its powerful stone archways to cleverly concealed secret panels, the illustrious castle captures a true feel of intrigue.

John Evans Brown first came to Asheville in the 1840s. Though he fell in love with the scenic Blue Ridge mountains, in 1849 he moved west to try his luck in the Gold Rush. After minimal success mining, he moved to New Zealand. There, Brown became a prominent legislator and sheep raiser. While serving in the Colonial Parliament, he even named his district "Swannanoa," after the Swannanoa River. Brown's sheep raising made him a very wealthy man and, in 1884, he returned to Asheville for good. Brown immediately began construction on his

courtesy the Ewart M. Ball Collection, Ramsey Library, UNC-Asheville

Zealandia as it originally appeared

massive home, overlooking the city below. He named the castle and the surrounding 168-acre estate "Zealandia" after his beloved second country.

John Evans Brown remained at Zealandia until his death, in 1895, at the age of 68. The castle was then sold by his heirs to O. D. Revel. Revel only kept the home a short while before selling it in 1904 to Sir Philip S. Henry. It was under the ownership of Henry that the castle became most widely known.

Sir Philip S. Henry, a native of Adelaide, South Australia, was a well known and prestigious scholar, traveler, and art patron. He was a member of the Pen and Plate Club, an elite literary and professional group in Asheville. He was also elected to the Academic Diplomatique Internationale of Paris. This honor was bestowed upon him for his service in the field of international education. At the time of his election, only three other Americans had ever been chosen for such an honor. By the time of his death, Henry possessed an incredible amount of distinguished international credentials. Due to his ownership of the home, many locals came to know Zealandia as "Henry's Castle."

It is interesting to note that just before Henry moved to Zealandia, his young wife, Violet Lewisohn, had died tragically in the infamous Windsor Hotel fire in New York City. The circumstances of her death are recounted by W. Vance Brown, the great grandson of John Evans Brown. "They got out... She went back in the hotel to get some pearls, I believe, or some jewelry she left in the room and it collapsed on her—she died that way." It is ironic that the factual death of a young woman by fire can be so closely related to the castle. If the classic legend of Helen is false, perhaps it was the retelling of this event that somehow con-

Bennett

Zealandia as it appears today

tributed to the present lore.

During Sir Philip S. Henry's twenty-nine-year stay at the castle, he was responsible for massive additions to Brown's original structure. Henry's extensive remodeling detracted from the castle-like look of the home to make it appear more "mansionesque." In one of the rooms of the lavish home was painted a medieval fresco that depicted actual people and places in the Asheville area at the time. The fresco even shows an image of what is believed to be Helen's Bridge. During this time span, President Calvin Coolidge considered an offer from Henry to use Zealandia as a summer White House.

Henry's renovations of Zealandia were the first of many the castle was to undergo. As time passed, almost every owner made some contribution to the structure of the building. Although in 1981 the castle stables accidentally burned down (a vagabond was trying to warm himself), no one can recall an earlier fire in which Helen's daughter may have been killed. Damage from such a fire would have surely been hidden by subsequent reconstruction, however.

Being an avid collector of art, Sir Henry dreamed of opening a museum to showcase his incredible collection. In 1930, his dream came true when Henry built and opened the Asheville Art Association and Museum on the estate property. The museum, open free to the public, housed rare pieces from around the globe. Man-sized vases from the Ming Dynasty rested side by side with original Renaissance paintings. For many years, thousands of Asheville residents and tourists enjoyed the magnificence of Henry's illustrious collection. However, in later years, the museum building would be de-

courtesy the Ewart M. Ball Collection, Ramsey Library, UNC-Asheville

*This photograph shows only a fraction of
Henry's illustrious art collection.*

Warren

*A fresco in one room of the castle depicts
what is believed to be Helen's Bridge*

stroyed in the construction of the Interstate 240 "open cut."

In 1933, while away in London, Sir Philip S. Henry died. The estate then passed into the hands of his two daughters, Violet and Lenore. The daughters married British military brothers named Maconochie. When Lenore's husband was killed in active duty, the widow sold her share of the castle to her sister and brother-in-law, Violet and General Hartley H. Maconochie. The Maconochies lived in the castle and, when their friend George Gershwin visited them, he composed part of his famous *Rhapsody in Blue* while a guest.

In 1961, the Maconochies sold Zealandia to George and Dottie Dixon, owners of the Sir William Hotel in Miami, Florida. The Dixons occupied the home in the spring while maintaining a winter home on Star Island in Miami Beach. The Dixons were art collectors as well. While one of the castle rooms housed the original thrones of the Emperor Maximilian and Carlota, Mrs. Dixon slept in the bed of Marie Antoinette.

Wayne Kinser, who presently leases Zealandia for his business, Peppertree Resorts, remembers Dottie Dixon's retelling of her first encounter with an apparition in the castle. The Dixons were casually seated in their television area one night when an apparition, in a black chiffon, glided down the main staircase, crossed the foyer, and then disappeared up the back staircase. The stunned Mrs. Dixon looked to her husband and asked, *"Did you see that?"* The wide-eyed man nodded in affirmation. Eager for an explanation, Mrs. Dixon called the Maconochies.

Their nonchalant answer was, as Kinser recounts, "Yes, that's Helen. She's looking for us—just tell her where we are."

"They did," Kinser said, "and Helen went away."

In 1969, George Dixon died. For four years, Mrs. Dixon lived in the large, mysterious castle all alone. Kinser remembers another of Mrs. Dixon's encounters with a ghost during this time. While in bed one night, she awoke to the sound of strange noises coming from beyond her locked bedroom door. In the shadows of the dark room, the door handle began to shake and rattle. Mrs. Dixon spoke calmly into the darkness. "George, now, I loved you when you were alive. But you're dead now, so go on where you belong and leave me alone." With that it stopped, and her husband's ghost never bothered her again.

There are other spooky stories which surrounded Zealandia during this period of time as well. It is said that sometimes the lonely Mrs. Dixon would light a candle and go wandering through the castle at night. As the old woman roamed throughout the dark and desolate corridors, the eerie glow of the candlelight passing by the windows could be seen from a distance. This sight alone might send chills up the spine of one accustomed to the castle's haunted legacy.

Zealandia is now the national headquarters for Wayne Kinser's business, Peppertree Resorts. Peppertree, a major time share developer, owns resorts across the nation. Over the years of land transactions, the Zealandia estate itself has been reduced to sixteen acres. The areas of the castle that were once bedrooms and living areas have now been converted into offices. Each day the castle bustles with the activity of dozens of employees. However, even with such activity, employees of the

Warren

*It can clearly be seen where the newer wooden structure
was added to the original stone base.*

castle still experience strange and haunting phenomena.

Gina Layne, who has worked in Zealandia for over two years, remembers the experience of a previous co-worker. The employee and another woman were working in the file room on the first floor of the building. Upon hearing a strange noise, the two turned around to find a continuous role of individual file folders springing, one by one, out of a drawer. There was no visible explanation for the display.

Layne herself has also experienced strange phenomena in the castle. While in the building late one evening, with no one else around, she heard what she believed to be pieces of mail flying out of the employee mailboxes. Layne was too frightened to cut a corner and examine the phenomenon visually. She was so shaken by the experience that she asked a friend to come to the castle and escort her upstairs.

As Layne recounts, "He had a beeper... As we were at the top of the steps, his beeper went off, and it showed all 'eights.' He said he normally got that when he had a low battery, but he had just put a new battery in. We went down a few steps, and it went off again and showed all 'eights.' And then, by the time we got to the end of the steps, his beeper went off all the way... He thought that was awfully unusual. That was a strange day for me, and I'll never come up here again by myself."

Gina Layne's sentiment is shared by many employees at Zealandia. It is not uncommon, for even an employee who has never had a strange experience, to have uneasy feelings about being in the castle alone.

Jim Harris worked alone in the castle at night for years. He single-handedly cleaned the building and pre-

Bennett

The burned out ruins of the old stables still stand today.

pared it for the following work day each evening. In all the time he worked such lonesome hours, he could only recall one strange occurrence. "I was on the second floor there, doing some work, and it sounded like a lady walked across the floor down there [on the first floor] in high heels. When I went to look there was no one there... That was probably a couple years ago."

Rumors of white forms and cold spots drifting throughout Zealandia abound. Whether the spirit in question is that of Helen, her daughter, or George Dixon is debatable. It is a fact, however, that documentably strange things do occasionally happen within the stately stone structure.

While investigating the castle, the author detected high bursts of electromagnetic energy that would inexplicably pass through some rooms. During one night of investigation, all the telephone lines in the building lit up simultaneously, blinked wildly, and then went off. Since this was late at night with only the research team and maintenance man around, there is no conventional explanation for the cause. One of the most provocative pieces of evidence, however, is a photograph the author took on Halloween night 1995, at approximately nine o'clock. The photograph, taken with 35mm film in the back lot of the castle, shows a large, white, shapeless mist hovering around a supply shed. The sight was not visible when the photo was taken. Such a photograph is, of course, typical of those associated with high amounts of electromagnetic activity.

As with most ghost stories, there are just as many skeptics as there are believers, when it comes to activity around Zealandia. There are naturally more people

*This photograph was taken by the author the night of
October 31, 1995, in the back lot of Zealandia. It was taken
in conjunction with massive fluctuations of electromagnetic
energy. Some say they can see a face formed by the mist,
especially when viewed from a distance. The mist was not
seen when the photograph was taken, however.*

who have never experienced anything than those who have. There are also other "haunted" places in the area to which the name Helen has been attached. In particular, there is a mountain in Arden called Helen's Mountain, where it is rumored that a Helen burned to death in a house fire.

We may never know the truth about who Helen really was. Was she the distraught mother, placed in a mindset that any parent could understand, who couldn't bear to live without her daughter? Was she the mistress, rejected and forlorn, who saw the answer to her problems while gazing off the bridge? Was her name coined from the ghastly murder of Helen Clevenger in the Battery Park Hotel? Or was she simply the figment of a campfire storyteller's imagination? We may never know the answers to these questions for sure. Still, however, strange things continue to happen on Beaucatcher Mountain.

The stories keep coming off the mountain of a phantom lady, searching for her daughter by the desolate roadside, and unexplainable lights and noises that emanate from the castle at night. And why does one get such a strange and gloomy feeling upon passing beneath the rafters of the looming bridge? Ghost or no ghost, it takes a truly brave soul to venture near the bridge when the moon is full, and the thick fog writhes and seethes among the mountains. And within this feeling, Helen shall always be present...yesterday... today... and tomorrow.

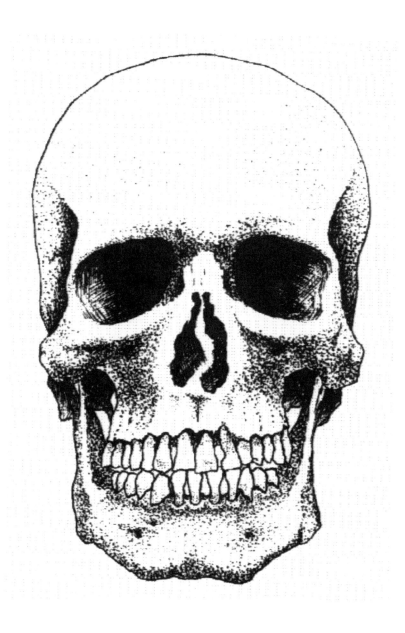

A
NIGHT OF TERROR
IN THE BUNCOMBE
COUNTY JAIL

U ntil now, you've read about the many different reactions that folks have to supernatural beings. Some have been impressed, some have been frightened, and others have even been comforted. Now, to sum up the spectrum of emotions, I offer you some grown men who were *absolutely terrified*. But even better than that, they were the toughest, meanest, most fearless men in Asheville—plus there was even a cage between them and the ghoul (or whatever it was). That's right, it was the men locked up in the Buncombe County Jail. The year was 1908, and somehow it seems that, as time has passed, the event has been all but forgotten. Although the jail house of that time period is now a vacant patch of land, what once happened there is unprecedented. Even though the men were scared senseless by what they experienced, it achieved what was, for them, the ultimate good. They "saw the light" that horrific night in the jail house, and accepted the Lord because of it. A tangible good came from what some may consider an intangible means. They had evidently seen a preview of hellfire in whatever visited them that April night.

What follows are actual reprints of two articles originally published in the *Asheville Gazette News* in 1908. They appear, in form and capitalization, just as they were printed. Enjoy...

Saturday, April 18, 1908

SPOOKS IN JAIL?
PRISONERS SCARED

A Ghostly Midnight Visitor— Rev. W. G. Whitaker Endeavored to Interview It.

'TWAS A FEARSOME SIGHT, SO EVERYONE TESTIFIES

Mr. Mitchell's Boarders Threaten to Leave Him in Most Unceremonious Manner.

Sheriff Hunter this morning received a communication from those unfortunate who occupy cells in the county jail, declaring that the window-barred house, just below the hill, was haunted, and pleading that work on the new jail be hastened that the prisoners might escape from the terrors that seize them nightly. This communication was the result of last night's experiences at the county jail, when the prisoners declare that a "spook" paid them a visit; that they saw "him" plainly; that "he" swung to and fro along the iron grating of the white cage from about midnight until near 2 o'clock this morning, and that the prisoners were well-nigh scared to death. In fact, it is declared by all the men in jail that two of the prisoners, Bob Boone and W. I. Miller fainted outright, while others, with the exception of "Rev." W.G. Whitaker, sought consolation, if not protection, beneath the folds of their blankets.

It was a wild-eyed bunch of prisoners that Jailor Mitchell found this morning about "feed time" when he entered the jail and, throwing the levers, allowed the prisoners the freedom of the cage corridors. Scarcely were the men in the corridors before they began relating to the jailor the night's experiences. That something unusual had taken place was evident and, as Mr. Mitchell listened to the tales told by the prisoners, corroborated one by the other, a sort of creepy feeling came over the strong and non-superstitious jailor and deputy sheriff. Boone and Miller were still badly frightened and weak. Other prisoners were in little better condition.

The story related to the jailor, and afterwards to others, had to do with the visitation of an alleged "spook." It is declared by all the prisoners in the white cage that about midnight they heard a noise, and subsequently there was a presence at the iron grating. An electric light is located in the jail near the cage, and the prisoners declare that they could plainly see the "presence": that is, the length of time they cast their eyes that way since— they were very frank about it—they just got one glimpse and then, in fright, sought the folds of their blankets, covering head and ears. All the prisoners performed this stunt with the exception of Rev. W. G. Whitaker, he who is the alleged representative of the Whitaker estate in England, and who is in jail in default of $2,500 bond, charged with using the mails for fraudulent purposes, in connection with the aforesaid Whitaker estate. The Rev. Mr. Whitaker was the hero of the occasion. He didn't hide his face, neither did he seek to flee from the "presence." He went forth and endeavored to speak with the "spook." But the prisoners declare that there was a "presence" at the bars and Rev. Mr. Whitaker corroborates them. He, with all the other prisoners in the cage, declare that the "presence" came about midnight and hung to the iron grating. They say it swung backward and forward, and grinned. It was when this grinning process commenced that the prisoners, with the exception of Mr. Whitaker, took to cover.

Whitaker declares that he sought to talk to the "spook," the "presence," or the "man"—whatever it was. He further says that it moved its lips but could not speak; that it poked its hand through the iron grating, and that every time it swung to the cage, it would grin in a manner calculated to make the hair stand. This thing continued for a time, and the negroes in the cage adjoining were awakened and became alarmed. All the negro prisoners, with the exception of Ben Johnson, did as the white prisoners and went to cover. Ben, like the Rev. Mr. Whitaker was a hero. He had the temerity to peep out and declares that what he saw made his blood run cold. He declares that the thing was just as the white men describe it; that it was a "spook" with great big eyes, and that it showed its teeth. The one peep was sufficient for Ben. He also went to cover and today declared that never again would he be a hero and take his head from cover when "spooks" are abroad in the land. It is said by the prisoners that the "presence" left about 2 o'clock as mysteriously as it came. They also declare that noises are heard in the jail at all hours of the night, and that the place is haunted. One night recently, the prisoners declare, they heard a mother and her babe crying "upstairs," and, furthermore, that almost every night they hear the "trap" fall; meaning by this the trap of the gallows on which a negro was recently hanged.

That there is something the matter at the jail is certain. Just what frightened the prisoners last night is not clear. They have appealed to Sheriff Hunter, however, urging that the new jail be completed as speedily as possible. Several of the prisoners this morning declared to Jailor Mitchell that while they "didn't intend to run over him" when he came to feed, that they just wanted to say they expected to "run past him" if ever the opportunity presented.

Monday, April 20, 1908

REFORM FOLLOWS VISIT OF SPOOK

Rev. Mr. Whitaker and the Other Prisoners Hold Hearty Religious Services in the Jail.

PRISONERS GIVE UP CARDS, PROFANITY IS ALSO TABOO

Miller, Alleged Robber, and Barnes, Alleged Horsethief, Prefers Conversion From Sinful Life.

Good has come of the Friday night incident at the county jail, when the prisoners confined there were so badly frightened by what they claim was the visitation of a "presence"—a "spook"—at the cage grating, which visitor, they said, remained at the cage and swung backward and forward for nearly two hours. It was about midnight Friday that the white prisoners say a "man" presented himself at the cage and grinned, and rolled his eyes, and licked out his tongue. Two of the prisoners were so badly frightened that they fainted, while all the others, with the exception of Rev. W. G. Whitaker, in jail in default of $2,500 bond, charged with using the mails for fraudulent purposes, went to their blankets, covering head and ears, and remaining thus until welcome daylight came.

Rev. Mr. Whitaker was not scared. He was so impressed, however, with the visitation that he sought to interview "it." He declares that the "presence" could not speak, but that "it" did move "its" lips and try to speak.

Saturday, the one topic of conversation among the prisoners in the jail, both black and white, had to do with the incidents of the night before and, when dark came on, many of the prisoners, still unnerved, became almost panic-stricken. They appealed to Rev. Mr. Whitaker to hold religious services. The preacher readily consented and, for two hours, the prisoners sang hymns and prayed, and listened to a Gospel talk by Mr. Whitaker.

The preacher prayed earnestly for the salvation of men, and especially for his fellow prisoners. He reprimanded his cell mates for their alleged wrongdoings, and pleaded with them to forsake their worldly and sinful ways, and seek and follow the lowly Nazarene.

The words of the preacher went home. A number of the prisoners were visibly affected, especially Will Miller, the man charged with robbing the post office at Arden, and who, on the night of the robbery, was run over by a train and had one of his feet crushed off, and James Barnes, one of the three men charged with stealing horses from Reems Creek township recently. Both of these men, at the conclusion of the services, went to Rev. Mr. Whitaker, shook hands with him, and declared their intention of accepting Christ and leading a better life. Will Miller told Jailor Mitchell Sunday morning that his life was completely changed. Mr. Mitchell says that it is a fact that Miller is now an entirely different man and prisoner; that he is now bright and happy instead of sullen, and of a rebellious nature. Rev. Mr. Whitaker, in speaking of the jail revival today, says that he has no regrets at being in jail; that he feels he has accomplished some good while there.

Mr. Mitchell said today that all the prisoners had evidently determined to live better lives. They handed Mr. Mitchell their playing cards yesterday, with the request that he burn up the little pieces of pasteboard. The prisoners have further made a rule that no more profanity or vulgar talk shall be indulged in.

=============================

Who says the Lord doesn't work in mysterious ways?

Meikle's photograph of the Jackson Building

THE BUILDINGS
HAVE EYES

On a final note, I shall leave you with a photograph that seems to speak for itself.

Around 1983, Robert Meikle, Jr., a photographer and enthusiast of local architecture, was taking some late night photographs of downtown Asheville. He decided to capture on film one of the city's most picturesque sites, the L.B. Jackson Building. Aside from the fact the photograph was taken late at night, the skyscraper was closed for renovations. This assured Meikle that no one was in or around the towering structure.

By the cadaverous light of a full moon, Meikle set his camera for a long exposure. As the film absorbed the surreal image, the photographer made certain there was absolutely no motion or interruption of the shot.

Later, when the photograph was developed, it was obvious that Meikle had captured a truly majestic image. However, he observed something else in his photograph that perplexed him endlessly. In the top, left-hand window of the tower, a strange form had also developed. Meikle was certain that it was not visible at the time the photograph was taken. To some, it appears to be a melancholy figure looking drearily at the city far below. Others have dismissed it as a simple glitch, or a trick of the light from the classic archways.

It wasn't long after the photograph was developed, however, that Meikle learned of a tragic story attached to the building. In the Great Depression, Asheville was hit especially hard. The Jackson building was not only the tallest in the city, but also a center of business. It is said that one fateful day, a hopeless victim of the economic disaster plunged to his death from a window of the Gothic structure. Since then, his restless soul has resided within the building in despair.

No one seems to know if there's any truth to the legend of the suicide. Obviously, though, it doesn't seem difficult to believe. It is surely possible that a mere glitch or trick of the light caused the mysterious form high in the top of the landmark. But then again, perhaps far above the gargoyles and archways, a dismal spectre overlooks the city of Asheville with otherworldly eyes.

If, while strolling through the city on some desolate night, as a full moon hovers above, you suddenly feel a stare on your back, turn around and let your gaze explore the windows of the antiquated buildings. Something may be watching from above—even if there's nothing to be seen.

For in Asheville, *the buildings have eyes.*

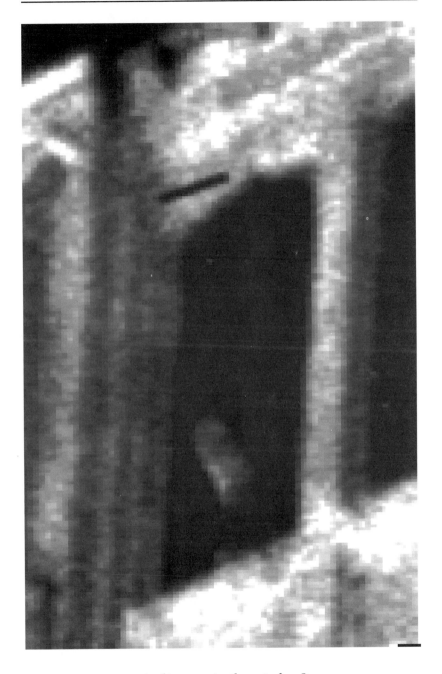

A phantom in the window?

INDEX

MARK-ELLIS BENNETT

Mark-Ellis Bennett has had a fascination with the paranormal as far back as he can remember. Mark assisted in the author's investigation of the Grove Park Inn by making photographic images that were receptive to only ultraviolet and infrared light. He furnished some equipment and participated in experiments employing Tesla Coils, Ion Generators, and ultra and subsonic audio recordings. Mark's biggest contribution was perhaps his ability as a sensitive, and his keen attention for detail.

Mark earned his Bachelor of Fine Arts degree at the Florida Atlantic University in Boca Raton. He also earned an Associate Degree in Culinary Science, has worked as a chef, and managed some rather impressive private clubs. After receiving the requirements needed to be awarded an Advanced Craft Certificate from the City and Guilds of London Institute, Mark has single-handedly undertaken some major restoration projects.

Mark has been self employed as a restoration craftsman and artist for four years, and in that capacity he has enjoyed continuous employment at the Grove Park Inn for most of that time. His remarkable work in the hotel has been featured in *Architectural Digest*. He remembers the Grove Park Inn from when his family first stayed there in 1963. "I have made many friends at Grove Park," he notes, "but before I met them, I had a sincere fondness for the inn, itself." Mark adds, "Whatever spirits may wander there, be they curious, protective, or even inclined to play small pranks, I have heard no recollections of a ghost that sets out to scare or harm anyone at Grove Park." Mark aspires to one day be curator to a property as fine as Asheville's Grove Park Inn.

TIM PEDERSEN

Tim Pedersen is no stranger to the arts. He began working on nationally distributed products while in his early teens. Before graduating from high school, he had already begun designing covers and illustrating books. Perfecting all from pen and ink to advanced computer graphics, Pedersen combines a unique feel of state-of-the-art technology with old-fashioned good taste. Aside from his numerous art awards and honors, his work has been nationally featured in *Computer Artist* magazine. Pedersen divides his time between the mountains of Asheville and the white shores of St. Petersburg, Florida.

ABOUT THE AUTHOR

Joshua P. Warren began writing his first published book, *Joshua Warren's Gallery of Mystery and Suspense*, at the age of thirteen. Since then, he has gone on to author more books and articles on a wide variety of subjects. He has written periodically for the *Asheville Citizen-Times* since 1992, and is the winner of several literary awards, including the University of North Carolina Thomas Wolfe Award for Fiction.

A member of the American Society for Psychical Research, Warren is also the President of LEMUR (the League of Etheric Materialization and Unexplained phenomena Research). This paranormal research team utilizes a number of investigative tools, including infrared and ultraviolet photography, ultra- and sub-sonic audio recording, electromagnetic field detection, and investigative journalism techniques. Through such research, Warren believes "the mysteries of today will yield the breakthroughs of tomorrow."

The President of Shadowbox Enterprises, as well as a lifelong resident of Asheville, Warren is an enthusiast of regional literature. He plans to publish more works of significance to Western North Carolina in the future.